JEWS BY CHOICE

A Study of Converts to Reform and Conservative Judaism

JEWS BY CHOICE

A Study of Converts to Reform and Conservative Judaism

Brenda Forster, Ph.D.
Department of Sociology
Elmhurst College
Elmhurst, Illinois

and

Joseph Tabachnik, Rabbi Emeritus
West Suburban Temple Har Zion
River Forest, Illinois

Ktav Publishing House, Inc.
Hoboken, New Jersey
1991

Library of Congress Cataloging-in-Publication Data

Forster, Brenda
    Jews by choice : a study of converts to Reform and Conservative
Judaism / Brenda Forster and Joseph Tabachnik.
        p.   cm.
    Includes bibliographical references.
    ISBN 0-88125-383-9
    1. Proselytes and proselyting, Jewish—Case studies.
2. Interfaith marriage—Illinois—Chicago—Case studies.   3. Reform
Judaism—Illinois—Chicago—Case studies.   4. Conservative Judaism-
-Illinois—Chicago—Case studies.   5. Jews—Illinois—Chicago—Case
studies.   I. Tabachnik, Joseph.   II. Title.
BM729.P7F67   1991
296.7'1—dc20   91-14555
                                                                              CIP

Dedicated to all those who have chosen to join the Jewish people and especially to all those who participated in our study.

—B. Forster

Dedicated in grateful recognition of Judd and Marjorie Weinberg, who helped make possible the publication of this book, and to my *Eshet Hayel*, Miriam, whose constant encouragement brought this volume to fruition.

—J. Tabachnik

TABLE OF CONTENTS

Preface

BACKGROUND TO THE BOOK

Only recently has the Jewish community placed the problem of conversion and of converts on its agenda. Converts to Judaism find themselves and their roles in the middle of a serious controversy about dangers to the continued existence of Judaism and of Jews. The debates on various aspects of the issues involving converts are passionate, heated, and complex. On one hand is the possibility of fracturing the religious community's unity over what is labeled the "Who is a Jew?" question. On the other hand is the equally intense debate over how to stop the advance of assimilation as increasing numbers of Jews become secular and then drop from the community that currently comprises only about 2.5 percent of the U.S. population. Added to the concern about dissolution of the community is the fact that even those Jews who are identified with the community seem to evidence a pattern of decline both in religious practice and in Jewish community involvement. Intermarriage between Jew and gentile is used by both optimists and pessimists to argue their view on predicting assimilation. Increasing intermarriage is seen by pessimists as an indication of continuing out-migration of Jews, and by optimists, looking to the increase in gentile conversions, as an indication of a needed infusion into the Jewish community. The issues of intermarriage and of converts are inexorably linked, since the majority of converts (more than 90 percent) are seriously involved with a Jewish partner at the time they seek conversion. As these philosophical and anecdotal debates rage, they are supported by meager statistics. Since only a handful of studies have focused on converts to Judaism, little is known about the actual roles and effects of converts in Judaism.

As a Conservative rabbi who participated in the development of the Introduction to Judaism course for potential converts to Judaism

xi

in the Chicago area, Rabbi Tabachnik found himself trying to defend the value of conversion and the positive contribution of converts. His synagogue drew many families with converts into its congregation, and as he saw the converts' growth and positive effects first hand, he became convinced of the need for a well-designed study to provide useful data on converts to the Jewish community. As a sociologist and as a convert to Judaism married to a convert, Dr. Forster had personally experienced some of the difficulties faced by converts and was keenly interested in documenting the experiences of converts. As a member of West Suburban Temple Har Zion, River Forest, Illinois, she had opportunities to interact with Rabbi Tabachnik. When asked, she readily agreed to collaborate with Rabbi Tabachnik on the study leading to this book.

In their joint endeavor, Rabbi Tabachnik made arrangements with the Chicago Association of Reform Rabbis and the Chicago Region of the Rabbinical Assembly, who since 1973 have jointly sponsored the Introduction to Judaism course for potential converts, to permit access to the addresses of past students and to classes enrolling students during 1987 and 1988. He made the resources of West Suburban Temple Har Zion available for mailing the questionnaires and convinced several members to volunteer their services to handle the mailings and to enter questionnaire data for computer analysis. He gained benefactors whose financial contributions supported the mailings and publication costs. He participated in designing the questionnaire and made various other contacts to aid the study's progress. And he took responsibility for researching information on biblical and rabbinical views about conversion. As part of his research, Rabbi Tabachnik gained a unique insight into a sociological principle that over the millennia seems to underlie the rabbis' decisions about the inclusion or exclusion of converts to the community.

Dr. Forster used her research and sociological skills to design the study, questionnaire, and data analysis formats. She drew on her experiences as a convert to develop the practical concerns that guide the approach of this book.

READER FOCUS

Early in the development of the study, we agreed that the book we would publish as one outcome of our study would be written to attract a wide readership, not just researchers or religious studies experts. Our concern was to provide a book that would not only present the specific findings of our study of current and former participants in the Introduction to Judaism course but also provide both sociological and religious contexts for the issues being debated. It is our hope that this book will interest born Jews, Jews by choice, intermarrieds, and prospective converts. As we previously indicated, the Jewish community is engaged in a debate about assimilation, intermarriage, and conversion. We hope this book will provide needed clarity to the facts and issues for born Jews who are directly involved as intermarrieds or as relatives of intermarrieds and for born Jews who are more indirectly involved as parties in the debate over the direction and form the community will take in the years to come. We also hope the book will aid those who have joined the Jewish community as intermarrieds, as converts, or as potential members. We perceive a need for non-Jews who attach themselves to the Jewish fold to understand the social and religious context in which their role is enacted. Understanding the Jewish community's concerns about the role of gentiles by birth should help highlight the issues converts and mixed-marrieds need to address if they desire a positive, committed, and useful attachment. Both groups, we hope, will find the data we provide interesting and beneficial.

Because we wish our material to be accessible to this wider audience of born Jews and of joiners, we have developed our presentation using easily understandable terminology and data formats. We do provide the reader with major references to aid further reading, but we have chosen to present ideas and themes rather than an extensive review of previous writings and research on our topics. We also provide chapter overviews and summaries so the reader will not lose track of the major concerns we will be addressing in our analysis.

STRUCTURE OF THE BOOK

The five chapters in this book are intended to lead the reader through the issues, to the data, and on to some practicalities that flow from this discussion. Chapter 1 introduces the U.S. Jewish community intermarriage situation and gives information on the patterns and controversies surrounding Jewish-gentile intermarriage and gentile conversion. This will provide a context for the reader to understand our data. Chapter 2 provides a synopsis of the four-thousand-year period (biblical and rabbinical) in which Jews have struggled with the role of outsiders who seek to join the Jewish family. We feel this information is needed both to provide a summary of rabbinical concerns and procedures that is not available elsewhere and to form the framework for analyzing and interpreting our data. Chapter 3 describes the study design and findings on the experiences of enrolled and former participants in the Introduction to Judaism course in Chicago, with an emphasis on actual converts to Judaism. Chapter 4 presents a comparison of main beliefs and practices of a sample of Reform and Conservative born Jews, the Jewish partners of the gentiles by birth, and the Introduction to Judaism participants. Chapter 5 gives a summary of the concerns raised throughout the book and offers our conclusions and recommendations. Tables to provide quick summaries of major points and of the data appear as needed throughout the book. It is our hope that the tables will be readable, interesting, and useful in their own right.

TERMINOLOGY

Before we proceed with our discussion, we need to explain something about the terminology we will be using throughout the book.

The words conversion and convert are actually gentile terms referring to a change in religious belief, identification, and practice. Particularly in Chapter 2, we will use various Hebrew terms that convey more the sense of identification with a people than with a religious system. The biblical term *ger* is the earliest designation of an outsider as "a stranger who resided in the midst of Jews;" later the term *ger zedek* (righteous alien-stranger) was applied to gentiles who identified with Judaism. The terms *proselyte* and *proselytism* are the concepts used officially in Jewish sources such as the *Encyclopedia Judaica*. The word *proselyte* comes from a Greek word meaning "to approach or to come to." And the terms conversion, proselytism, and missionizing primarily refer to the process of a religious community seeking to make members of outsiders. The latter two terms convey an active outreach by the community to "entice" outsiders to join. Added to these various terms used to describe the person and the process of gaining group membership is the recently coined term *Jew by choice*, which some prefer to the term convert.

Another set of terms referring to marriage between Jews and gentiles causes problems in understanding for outsiders. The terms reflect the ambivalent attitude toward themselves that converts encounter in the Jewish community. In Christian circles, a person from outside the faith or denomination who converts is considered a full member, loses all former identifications, and when counted is considered a Catholic, or Baptist, or Lutheran, or whatever. And when that person marries an insider, the marriage is considered of one faith, not as an interfaith marriage. Not so in Judaism, as we will discuss in more detail in Chapter 1. Marriages between a convert to Judaism and a Jew are still considered intermarriages by Jews. Only occasionally and in technical discussions is a distinction recognized between mixed intermarriages in which the gentile spouse does not convert and conversionary intermarriages in which the gentile spouse converts to Judaism.

We have elected to use the term *gentile* in our discussion as the category for all those not born Jews, though occasionally we use the term non-Jew. We are aware that they are generalization terms that mask many potentially important distinctions among out-group members; that is, some gentiles may be more acceptable to Jews than others, some more attracted to Judaism than others. But such distinctions are not our concern here. We felt that the term *gentile* was less judgmental and more universally used than the term *non-Jew*. We also focus our discussion on Jewish-Christian (mainline Protestant and Catholic) relationships because the majority of U.S. intermarriages with Jews are with spouses from Christian backgrounds. There are Jewish-Moslem, Jewish-Hindu, Jewish-Buddhist, and other such unions, but they are scarce, and little is known of them. Generally speaking, Jewish-gentile intermarriages are racially homogenous—white. (In the United States, Semites of northern European extraction are considered white.) An estimated 6 percent of Jewish-Gentile conversionary unions are racially mixed (black, oriental, Asian, Indian, Hispanic, and so on); two-thirds of these partners convert to Reform Judaism because of its outreach efforts (Gallob, 1990). Again, little is known of these special situations. Therefore, our discussion addresses the majority intermarried situation of born Jew with a white, Christian, gentile spouse who may be a convert to Judaism.

In speaking of gentiles who seek attachment to a born Jew and/or Judaism, we will use several terms including *non-Jewish partner, gentile spouse, potential convert,* and *student.* We also use the terms *out-marriage, mixed marriage,* and *intermarriage* basically interchangeably to refer to Jewish-gentile marriages, since all these terms are used in the literature. *Out-marriage* is more commonly used by sociologists along with the term *exogamous; intermarriage* is the more generally used term.

Another point to which the reader should be alerted and that we discuss in our subsequent chapters is the need to address both a religious and an ethnic dimension in the relationship of the gentile within the Jewish community. To a Christian, the focus of conversion is a religious one. Religious conversion in a marriage context is an accepted model among religious Christians. Only in vague notions of close family bonds and Jewish cohesiveness with perhaps a bit of awareness of Jewish humor does a modern U.S. gentile generally apprehend the ethnic domain that is as important to Jewish identity and definition as religious practice, perhaps more so. It is relatively easier for a sincere gentile to practice Judaism than it is to be a recognized and respected member of the Jewish community. It is difficult for a gentile to absorb ethnic empathy, commitment, and self-identification, to speak of we, us, and our when speaking of Jews. We trace the long-term Jewish concern with both dimensions in the discussion that follows. In order to make clearer what we will call the ethnic, cultural, or peoplehood domain, Figure 2.1, pages 49–50, provides a brief summary of major differences between U.S. Jews and the Christian gentile majority. Most of the differences are ethnic (sociocultural) in nature.

Generally for simplicity we will use the term *Jews* and *Jewish community* in our discussions. However, historically the ancestors of the people now called Jews have been variously called by themselves and by others—for example, Israelites, Hebrews, tribes, and sons of the Patriarchs. Modern Jewish issues are rooted in the experiences of these ancestors, and in Chapter 2 we discuss historical differences and changes for each of the major periods as the Jewish people evolved. We also speak of Judaism, which is a religious identification fostered by the rabbis in diaspora (the exiled or by-choice life of Jews outside the land of Israel). The modern religion of Judaism contains only prayers as correlates of the earlier sacrificial religion. Other religious identifications usually applied by outsiders have focused on the people as worshipers of the One God, as People of the Covenant, as Chosen People (chosen by God for his personal Revelation), and as People of the Book. When we speak of religious leaders and experts, we acknowledge the fact that the rabbis have built their rulings on the traditions of the prophets before them, who built on the work of the priests, and judges, who gained inheritance from Moses and the Patriarchs. In identifying the various time periods involved in the development of the Jewish people and Judaism, we will use the abbreviations BCE (Before the Common Era) and CE (Common Era) rather than the Christian-oriented BC (Before Christ) and AD (Year of the Lord).

Another consideration for the reader and for converts especially is the difference between Christians and Jews in emphasis on beliefs and behavior. Christians stress issues of belief as central to their relationship to God while Jews stress actions as a member of a covenantal community. Religiously oriented Christians who seek to learn about Judaism whether in the writings of Jews or through courses such as Introduction to Judaism find discussions on the proper rituals for observing the holidays but precious little about Jewish tenets. Jews do have beliefs that can be characterized as theological, but traditionally these beliefs are implicit in action-oriented considerations. In introducing new members to the faith community, Jews begin with the history (experiences and practices) of Jews from Abraham to the present while Christians begin with faith (belief) propositions based on the death and resurrection of the person they call Christ. We will discuss the relevance of the practice versus belief emphasis further in Chapters 3 and 4.

The reader may also notice that our spelling of Hebrew terms is different from spellings used elsewhere. Transliteration (representation of Hebrew letters and pronunciations in English) is not standardized. For example, the world *Hanukah* is also spelled *Hanukkah, Chanukah,* and *Chanukkah* depending on the source. We have tried to use the simplest and most common form and then stick to it for consistency. We also italicize all but the most commonly known Hebrew terms.

Finally, we will use the term *assimilation* to refer to the adherence of born Jews to the larger gentile culture, which in the extreme means that either they or their children lose their identities as Jews. We will use the term *absorption* to refer to the integration of gentiles into the Jewish community in such a way that either they or their children become fully recognized and participate as Jews.

With these complexities in mind, we proceed with our discussion.

READER ISSUES

In reading the pages that follow, the reader may wish to ponder the following questions:

- In what context have issues of assimilation into the gentile community versus absorption of gentiles into the Jewish community arisen over the years?
- What is similar and what is different about the modern U.S. context of concerns about intermarriages and conversion and other periods?
- What procedures for admission of gentiles to Judaism have been established over the millennia?
- What behaviors are expected of converts in the religious domain and in the ethnic (sociocultural) domain?
- What are the religious and ethnic beliefs and behaviors evidenced by converts to Judaism?
- How do the beliefs and practices of converts to Judaism compare with born Jews, with their Jewish spouses, and with gentiles who intermarry without conversion to Judaism?
- What concerns should the current U.S. Jewish community address if it wishes to aid the absorption of converts, including their Jewish identification and participation?
- What issues need to be addressed if the children of Jewish-gentile intermarriages are to identify and involve themselves as Jews and to pass that participation on to their children?

ACKNOWLEDGEMENTS

A project of this size requires the support of many people, not just the authors. The Chicago Association of Reform Judaism and the Chicago Region of the Rabbinical Assembly, who jointly sponsor the Introduction to Judaism course, provided us access to both former and current students. We had the help of pretesters, born Jews, Jewish partners, and current and former students in the Introduction to Judaism course who were gracious enough to take the time needed to answer our lengthy questionnaire. We had office help from the staff of West Suburban Temple Har Zion, River Forest, Illinois, to organize and conduct our mailing. Both Doris Levin and Lucy Matz became involved as staff members. We were blessed with the volunteer help of several members of West Suburban Temple Har Zion to complete our mailing operation. Bernice Sheft spent hours and hours as the manager of the mailing operation. With the help of various women in the temple, Bernice completed the exacting task of tracking down current names and addresses of former students; folding, stuffing, and labeling the questionnaire mailings;

keeping records on returns; and doing follow-up mailings. Barry Weiss used his computer services to prepare our mailing labels. Maxine Horwich spent months entering the questionnaire data onto computer disks for entry to our computer. Russel Forster, Brenda's son, acted as research assistant and data processor. His knowledge and skill at running the SPSSX package on the Harris 800 system at Elmhurst College got the massive amount of data we obtained into shape. Kari Busch aided the work in transcribing the data from printouts to summary sheets. Rita Kuta, Brenda's sister, provided the needed word processing expertise to prepare the various questionnaries and manuscripts. We are also indebted to David Stadt and to Miriam Tabachnik for their support.

The librarians at Spertus College of Judaica, Chicago, particularly Dan Sharon and Yehoshua Ben Avraham, aided us in finding the necessary sources for our discussions in Chapter 1 and Chapter 2. Dr. Monford Harris and Dr. Byron Sherwin, also of Spertus College, read early drafts of portions of this book and gave invaluable suggestions.

A special recognition goes to Rabbi William Frankel of Northfield, Illinois, whose knowledge of rabbinics and keen perception of American Jewish life influenced our thinking.

Finally, without the generous financial contributions of Judd and Marjorie Weinberg and Alvin Gottlieb this project would not have gotten off the ground. We acknowledge with gratitude that their generosity supported the questionnaire, data analysis, manuscript preparation, and publication phases for this book. We are indeed fortunate that they believed in the importance of this endeavor and were willing to underwrite much of this project.

To all who aided us, we extend our appreciation.

1

Patterns and Issues of U.S. Jewish-Christian Intermarriage and of Gentile Conversion to Judaism

FROM THE POINT of view of the Jewish community, intermarriage of Jews with gentiles is the main concern and not conversion. As we indicated in the Preface, even where there is conversion of the gentile partner to Judaism, Jews still consider the marriage an intermarriage. Therefore, while our book is about converts, we have to begin with a discussion of Jewish concerns about intermarriage in order to understand their reaction to conversion and to converts.

In this chapter we will examine trends of intermarriage in the United States. Then we will turn our attention to current U.S. trends in conversion to Judaism. This discussion will provide the context for the concerns to which our study responds.

TRENDS IN U.S. JEWISH INTERMARRIAGE

To get some idea of the importance of and effect of Jewish intermarriage in the United States, one must look at the historical patterns and trends. The data presented here are drawn from a mixed bag of sources—government statistics, local Jewish community studies, and a few national studies. Since the data are spotty and often not easily comparable, one must use great caution not to take the numbers as absolute. At the same time, the data suggest patterns and trends and are all that is available. Eleven major Jewish community studies tend to be cited in the literature: Los Angeles 1986, Denver 1981, American Jewish Committee (Egon Mayer)

1

1976, National Jewish Population Study 1971, Boston 1965, Providence 1963, NORC 1961, Indiana 1959, San Francisco 1958, Washington 1956, and Iowa 1953. Only three of these studies used a national sample, and the Indiana and Iowa data are from government data on rather small, atypical Jewish populations. In the discussion that follows, we will give the data source only when it is particularly relevant. Most of the published reports on the Jewish community and on intermarriage provide pattern information and estimates of trends without giving the data source. In addition, estimates from different studies vary somewhat in their projection of patterns.

The first U.S. Jewish intermarriage was recorded in 1660, only six years after Jews first came to New Amsterdam (Mayer, 1985, p. 78). Because of an unbalanced sex ratio in the colonial period, it is estimated that from 1776 to 1840 the intermarriage rate was 28.7 percent (Stern, 1967, pp. 142–143). However, once there was an influx of Jewish immigrants in the early 1900s, the rate dropped to 1.2 percent. From 1900 to 1940, the intermarriage rate was 2 percent to 4 percent, and from 1940 to 1950 it was 5 percent to 6 percent (Silberman, 1985, p. 287). Until the 1960s, the intermarriage rate for Jews was below 10 percent. A study by Rosenthal (1963) of Iowa data indicated that Jews in small Jewish communities had a considerably higher rate of intermarriage than those in concentrated communities (36.3 percent in 1953 and 53.6 percent in 1959).

By the late 1950s, while Jewish centers had lower intermarriage rates than small communities, their rates were also increasing. The Washington study in 1956 showed a 13.1 percent intermarriage rate of which 9.4 percent were Jewish males out-marrying and 4.5 percent were Jewish females (Rosenthal, 1963, p. 16). By 1965 in Boston the rate had risen to 20 percent (Schwartz, 1970, p. 110), and by the early 1970s the estimates were of a 32 percent rate (Mayer and Sheingold, 1979, p. 2). Interestingly, the 1986 Los Angeles study showed a 20.2 percent rate (17 percent to a Christian partner, 3.2 percent to partners of other backgrounds) (Sandberg, 1986, p. 53). It appears that while the intermarriage rate has been increasing overall, currently it is about one-fifth (20 percent) rather than the commonly accepted one-third (33 percent).

A qualification to this lower figure must be made, however. The 20 percent rate represents an average of all generations. Some research indicates that the rate varies by generation. Sandberg found in the Los Angeles study that the first generation (foreign-born) intermarriage rate was 11.6 percent, the children of immigrants had a 12.7 percent rate, the third generation rate was 28.8 percent, and the fourth generation rate was 43.5 percent (1986, p. 140). Since Los Angeles has a large Jewish community, the finding of an almost 50 percent intermarriage rate for great-grandchildren of immigrants is unsettling, since that generation is both large and influential in determining the future for the Jewish community. Even more alarming, a 1988 study by social scientists at Brandeis University found an out-marriage rate of 72 percent for current eighteen- to twenty-nine-year-old Jews (Gallob, 1988, p. 27).

As a comparison, the rate of Jewish intermarriage, while of great concern to the Jewish community, has remained well below the intermarriage rates for other religious and ethnic groups. In 1957, a voluntary population survey conducted by the U.S. government showed 7.2 percent of existing marriages in which one marital partner was Jewish and the other gentile, whereas 21.5 percent of those involving Catholics were interdenominational intermarriages. The rate for Protestant interdenominational marriages was 8.6 percent in the 1930s (Baron, 1952) but was 30 percent to 40 percent by the 1950s. Today out-marriage rates for Christians (marrying across denominations) is greater than 50 percent. The comparatively lower rate for Jews, which was maintained for a longer period than for other religious groups (20 percent to 30 percent for Christian groups by the 1950s but not until the 1980s for Jews), reflects stronger ethnic-family-peoplehood ties present in the Jewish community than in the Christian community. However, because of their significantly smaller size, losses of members are a more serious threat to the continued survival of a Jewish community in the United States and worldwide. Therefore, Jews show greater concern than do Christian groups about the effect of loss of members. Christian denominations also have the advantage that out-marriage of their members is to other Christian denominations. So, for example, loss of a Catholic in marriage to a Lutheran is still not a loss for Christendom, whereas marriage of a Jew to a Christian is more likely to lead to a permanent loss for the Jewish community. We will return to this issue in the next section.

Consequently, a 7.2 percent loss rate in the late 1950s, though low by today's standards, began to agitate some in the Jewish community. The figure had doubled since the immigrant generation. In December 1964, the Commission on Synagogue Relations and the Federation of Jewish Philanthropies in New York sponsored a conference on "Intermarriage and the Future of the American Jew." Significantly, only some of the participants mentioned the possibility of initiating programs so gentile partners could convert; the others outlined programs on prevention. In a summary of the proceedings, Graenum Berger spoke about "arresting" and "preventing" intermarriage (1964, p. 159).

As the rate of intermarriage increased significantly in the 1960s, data from the "National Jewish Population Study," conducted by the Council of Jewish Federation and Welfare, were released in 1971. The findings stunned the Jewish community. From 1961 to 1965, the rate of intermarriage had risen to 17.4 percent, and, from 1966 to 1971, by some widely accepted estimates the rate had climbed to 31.7 percent. (Though, as we previously stated, some experts believe a 20 percent rate to be a more accurate estimate.)

The steep increase was due to many factors. It seems that Jews had completed the naturalization process begun by the immigrant generation and, therefore, had shed their immigrant ties. The sharp increase in intermarriage was also the result of other factors in the American environment. The civil rights struggle and subsequent legislation enacted by Congress in 1964 forbade discrimination in employment, and the quota systems in universities that discriminated against Jews were abolished, while corporations opened their doors to minority groups including Jews. Jews left their parental homes and began to enroll in universities that had been closed to them previously; many joined corporate life, which entailed mobility. The feminist revolution opened careers for women that made it possible for them to lead a less sheltered existence that, in turn, led to broader socialization with people of the opposite sex.

The memories of Christian persecution, so traumatic to the older generation, were no longer relevant to many young people. Jews acquired gentile friends and began to experience an openness in American life. The church likewise began to encourage an openness to other faiths. Pope John XXIII, after Vatican II, which, according to him, "opened a window to the world," urged the church to increase interdenominational contacts that included Jews and to broaden social contacts.

In view of these pressures toward greater intermarriage, the Jewish community could no longer ignore the possibility of attrition due to intermarriage. What to do about it become an item of priority of the Jewish agenda.

In 1973, Rabbi Schindler, the president of the Union of American Hebrew Congregations, the lay body of the Reform movement, called for "a positive effort to come to grips with the problem of intermarriage, to contain the loss of our numerical strength which it threatens, and, if at all possible, to convert the loss into a gain." With concern for the next generation of Jews, Schindler called for attempts to ensure "that the majority of the children issuing from such marriages, will in fact be reared as Jews. . . . We need to stop bemoaning our fate, to shake off once and for all the defensive stand, born out of a ghetto mentality, and to make Judaism a proud and assertive faith."

Intermarriage does not occur without prior dating contact, since in the United States people use dating as the mechanism for mate selection. Sandberg found differences in teen out-dating depending on Jewish religious affiliation as follows: Orthodox 39 percent, Conservative 62 percent, and Reform 67 percent. These rates increase somewhat to 51 percent, 74 percent, and 85 percent for Jewish individuals no longer living with their parents. Los Angeles Jews showed little resistance in their stated reactions should their own child intermarry. Intermarriage for their own child was opposed by only 38 percent of the Orthodox, 16 percent of Conservatives, and 12 percent of the Reform congregants (Sandberg, 1986, p. 54). As our later discussion will show, this acceptance of intermarriage is a rather new phenomenon and certainly gives doomsayers a basis for their prophecies.

Having looked at the patterns in intermarriage, we briefly turn our attention to a further specification of the vital issues intermarriage raises for the Jewish community.

ISSUES FOR THE JEWISH COMMUNITY ABOUT INTERMARRIAGE

Intermarriage has been viewed as a perennial danger to Jewish validity and continuity (Rosenman cited by Silberman, 1985, p. 286).

Intermarriage is a holocaust of our own making (Rabbi Sol Roth cited by Silberman, 1985, p. 286).

The hydra-headed monster of assimilation takes on many forms, the most menacing of which is intermarriage (Robert Gordis cited by Silberman, 1985, p. 285).

The topic of Jewish intermarriage (especially of Jewish-Christian intermarriage, the most frequent kind) and the related subtopic of conversion and of converts to Judaism touches a root nerve in the Jewish psyche. Intermarriage is invariably tied to intense fears of the demise of the Jewish community through assimilation into the dominant culture. Intermarriage, according to the worst scenario, is the next to last step for Jews moving out of the Jewish community.

Recent discussions reflecting on the survival chances of the Jewish community seem to fall into one of two camps—assimilationists/pessimists or transformationists/optimists (Glazer, 1987, p. 14). The pessimists claim that trends associated with modernism, secularization, and assimilation will cause the demise of the Jewish community in the United States over the next several decades. They point to several demographic indicators. The percentage of Jews in the U.S. population is falling. In 1880, Jews were 0.5 percent of the U.S. population, in 1930 3.7 percent, but in 1984 2.5 percent (approximately 5.5 million). This now falling percentage is affected by a decrease in Jewish immigration to the U.S. (even Russian immigration is now redirected to Israel), a falling Jewish birth rate (1.5 in 1965 and 0.7 in 1975) that is well below even replacement level, and a rising intermarriage rate (7 percent in the 1940s, 17 percent in the 1960s, and an estimated 20 percent to 32 percent in the 1980s) (Goldstein, 1987, p. 131). Add to these decreases the rising mortality rate of an aging Jewish population and the "passing" of an unknown number of born Jews to whom identify as a Jew is meaningless at best and a detriment at worst. (Orthodox commentators would include the "falling away" from *halachic* Judaism of Conservative, Reform, and Reconstructionist Jews as also indicting steps toward the demise of the Jewish community.) Most pessimists also include the lack of intensive Jewish education for the majority of Jewish children and delay of marriage in twenty-five to thirty-four-year-olds (98 percent married in the 1960s, 74 percent in the 1970s) (Goldstein, 1987, p. 137). (A delay in marriage is also associated with lower birth rates.) In the 1960s Sklare was one of the first to sound the alarm about the decreasing U.S. Jewish population. He particularly pointed to intermarriage as the main problem, because,

> in its collective aspects intermarriage menaces the continuity of the group. In its individual aspects, it menaces the continuity of generations within the family, the ability of family members

to identify with one another, and the satisfaction of such members with their family roles (Sklare, 1971, p. 182).

The optimists, on the other hand, while viewing similar data, come to different conclusions about the future for the Jewish community and about the meaning and effect of intermarriage. For the optimists, while the Jewish population is proportionally decreasing, 5.5 million is still a large community. They point to recent evidence that fourth-generation Jews desire larger families than their parents and to the fact that a high education and occupational status no longer means a decrease in family size. (Unlike their gentile counterparts, upper status Jewish females have larger than replacement-size families.) While optimists agree that intermarriage is a factor to be considered, they believe the actual rates to be about 24 percent (Silberman, 1985, p. 293), and they point out that some 20 percent to 50 percent of gentile spouses eventually convert to Judaism (one-third is the usually accepted estimate). According to Mayer, the major researcher on intermarriage, the rate of conversion to Judaism went up 300 percent during the last twenty years but may now be falling (1983, p. 58). During the 1970s, some 7,000 to 8,000 people per year converted to Judaism, with Jews by choice comprising an estimated 2 percent to 4 percent (about 100,000) of all Jews. Optimists believe these "imports" counterbalance losses to the community. The optimists argue that while there has been a decrease in traditional Jewish practices by most Jews, there is near universal observance of Passover and Hanukah, a very high participation in Rosh Hashanah and Yom Kippur, and a strong commitment to Israel (Glazer, 1987, p. 14). Three-fourths of Jews still identify with a "denomination" (Goldscheider, 1987, p. 278), and most Jews indicate that the majority of their friends are Jews. According to one optimist:

> The Jewish community in America has changed, indeed has been transformed [by modernization]. But, in that process, it has survived as a dynamic source of networks and resources binding together family, friends, and neighbors, ethnically and religiously—in every way the American Jewish community represents for Jews and other ethnic minorities a paragon of continuity and change in modern pluralistic society (Goldscheider, 1987, p. 280).

In sum, the controversy over intermarriage then represents the core concern of the Jewish community, which lost one-third of its members recently in the Holocaust. Is intermarriage the final step before assimilation? Do conversionary intermarrieds contribute to the strengthening or to the dissolution of the practice of Judaism and of Jewish identity? What about the offspring of intermarrieds—are they lost to the Jewish community? We hope our study will shed some light on these questions.

Having looked at the patterns of Jewish intermarriage and having considered the issues those patterns raise, we turn our attention to the specific concern of this book—conversion to Judaism. What do we know about the patterns in conversion to Judaism?

TRENDS IN U.S. CONVERSIONS TO JUDAISM AND IN INTERMARRIAGE IDENTITY

As debates and concerns about Jewish intermarriage have arisen, another change has complicated the Jewish-gentile intermarriage picture—conversion to Judaism by the gentile (usually Christian) partner. Although the first conversion in the United States took place in 1763 in Philadelphia (Mayer, 1985, p. 90), before the 1960s conversion to Judaism by the gentile partner was exceedingly rare. By the 1980s, Mayer and others estimate that about one-third of the gentile spouses are converting to Judaism, while another 20 percent, although they do not convert, still identify themselves as Jewish (1987, p. 90). Ten percent of the Jewish spouses convert to their gentile partner's religion, and 17 percent reject all religious identity (Mayer, 1987, p. 214). While this latter 27 percent are lost to the Jewish community, the remaining three-quarters of intermarrieds retain ties and identification with Judaism and the Jewish community.

The 1961 NORC study calculated an intermarriage loss rate according to the partner's religious identity. It was found that in Protestant-Jewish marriages, 66 percent of the Jewish male partners and 58 percent of the Jewish female partners retained their identity, producing a loss rate of 20 percent; Catholic-Jewish intermarriages produced retention rates of 62 percent and 53 percent, respectively, or a Jewish loss rate of 26 percent. In intermarriages where both partners disavow a religious identification, 38 percent of the Jewish males and 50 percent of the Jewish females retain an ethnic Jewish identity with a loss rate of 47 percent. Overall, 55 percent of Jews intermarrying retain their Jewish identification (Schwartz, 1970, p. 112). It is the larger group of Jewish-identified conversionary couples that we will focus on in our subsequent discussion.

According to Mayer, for the one-third of gentile partners who convert to Judaism, 15 percent convert before meeting their partner, 40 percent convert before marriage, 23 percent convert before the birth of the first child, and 22 percent convert at other times (1985, p. 235). Mayer also indicates that partners of a Catholic background are least likely to convert, then those with no religious identity, then those from a Protestant faith, and most likely to convert are liberal Protestants whose own parents were part of an intermarriage (1985, p. 230). Ninety percent of converts to Judaism are females (Mayer as quoted by Gallob, 1985, p. 20). As we shall see in Chapter 3, our data show similar patterns.

In an attempt to distinguish the various combinations of intermarrieds, the terms *mixed* and *conversionary* or *mitzvah* marriages are used. As we previously stated, it should be noted here that other religious groups do not consider couples as intermarried when the nonmember converts. The Jewish community, however, is uncomfortable about converts, not accepting them as "real" Jews and expressing concern as to how much they will "water down" Jewish practices and/or import Christian or other observances into the marriage. Consequently, the term *intermarried* is used for all couples where one partner was not born Jewish. Mayer proposed four categories of intermarrieds: (1) Assimilationists (10 percent), where the born Jew converts to the partner's religion; (2) Rejectionists (17 percent), where the partners reject any religious identity; (3) Conversionist (33 percent), where the gentile converts to Judaism; and (4) Integrationist (40 percent), where neither partner converts, but they try to blend observances from both backgrounds (1985, p. 282). The chart in Figure 1.1 graphically presents these various combinations of intermarriage.

SUMMARY OF PATTERNS AND ISSUES

To summarize, the data indicate that the general Jewish intermarriage rate has increased since 1960 from less than 10 percent to about 20 percent (some say 32 percent). The rates are higher for native-born generations, with the fourth generation showing almost a 50 percent rate. In the past, it was primarily Jewish males who

FIGURE 1.1
VARIATIONS IN FORMS OF JEWISH INTERMARRIAGE

Inter-marriage Type	Mixed				Conversionary	
Religious Identity	Jew by birth-Gentile No Religious Identity	Christian-Jew Separate Identifications*	Christian-Jew Identifying with Jews	Christian-Jew Convert to Christian**	Jew-Christian Convert to Judaism with Christian Leanings	Jew-Christian Convert to Judaism Fully Jewish-Oriented
Mayer Percentage	17%	20%	20%	10%	33%	
Mayer Term	Rejectionist	Integrationist		Assimilationist	Conversionist	

* We use Christian here for convenience since the majority of intermarriages are Jew-Christian. The categories apply to other religious identifications such as Buddhist-Jew and so on.

** This category is not usually studied since the Jewish community does not consider an out-convert part of the group.

out-married, but currently the ratio of Jewish males to Jewish females out-marrying is nearly equal. Interdating is a growing practice even among Orthodox Jews. Younger Jews of all branches show little rejection of intermarriage for their own children. These patterns suggest serious problems afoot for maintaining the U.S. Jewish community at its current number of 5.5 million.

A possible countering factor is the fact that about one-third of the gentile spouses eventually convert, another 20 percent consider themselves Jews without formal conversion but by commitment, and another quarter seek to maintain some kind of Jewish identity and practice along with the gentile spouse's religion. Only about 20 percent of intermarrieds completely reject Judaism and a Jewish identity. Most converts are females from a liberal Protestant background converting to Reform Judaism.

The various combinations of intermarried identifications are, for simplicity, usually discussed as either mixed or conversionary, which we will do also.

We have shown the matter of Jewish intermarriage to be related to key identity and survival issues for the entire Jewish community. As the rate of out-marriage has continued to increase, Jewish response generally has moved from total rejection, to grudging acceptance, to resignation, and to growth in attempts to react in a positive manner as gentile spouses began to seek conversion in greater numbers.

Before we continue analyzing the issues about the role of converts using our study data, we will turn our attention to rabbinic concerns and policies for conversion over the centuries. Since converts today gain legitimate Jewish identification only through a religious conversion handled by a rabbi, it is imperative that we understand this religious context. It is the rabbis who debate and decide the criteria for admission. To their point of view we now turn our attention.

2

Rabbinic Concerns and Rulings about Conversion to Judaism

INTRODUCTION

We will let the words of the biblical convert Ruth—"Your people shall be my people"—provide the question for our discussion: For Jews, how does "your people become my people?" We begin our investigation of the meaning and process of conversion to Judaism with an examination of the concerns and the procedures established by the rabbis and their precursors. We will be examining a four-thousand-year span in which outsiders became one with the Jewish people.[1]

The discussion of conversion occurs in several major sources—the biblical text itself, various segments of the Talmud, codes, responsa, philosophical literature, and most recently in various rabbinic writings. These various sources will serve as guidelines to our understanding of the problems associated with accepting converts to Judaism. A catalog of the various writings actually leads to what appears to be contradictory decisions—some in favor, some opposed to accepting converts. However, the prevailing notion in our culture today is that Judaism throughout history discouraged proselytism and conversion, a view colored by the influence of the last two thousand years, which have tended to make conversion a difficult process, as we shall see. Since other writers have sought to gather comprehensive information about rulings concerning conversion to Judaism, it is our intention to provide only a summary overview. Two important works on the topic are *Jewish Proselytism in the*

---

1. For simplification we will talk about conversion to Judaism even when we are incorporating the earlier situations of joining the tribes, the Hebrews, and the Israelites.

First Five Centuries of the Common Era (Braude, 1940) and *Proselytism in the Talmudic Period* (Bamberger, 1939).

As we began to research for this book we agreed that we needed a framework in order to make sense of the various authoritative opinions and to aid our data analysis as well. As we looked at the rabbinic sources, we began to see a common, transcending theme. Whether the procedures for joining the Jewish people (including intermarrying) were severe or lenient seemed consistently related to concerns (or lack of them) about the community's ability to absorb outsiders into the group. To make it clear, our conclusion is as follows:

> In times when intermarriage tended to lead to the assimilation of Jewish partners into the gentile world, such marriages were strongly discouraged, and the requirements for conversion became demanding.
>
> In times when conditions tended to ensure that the gentile partner would be absorbed by the Jewish community, requirements for conversion were lenient or absent.

Given this rather sociological view of the issue of conversion, our following account and analysis will address three primary concerns for each of the major periods—biblical, talmudic, posttalmudic, and modern. The three issues are: (1) What is the sociohistoric context of the Jewish community, particularly as it relates to the concern about absorption/assimilation? (2) What specific concerns about absorption/assimilation are illustrated? and (3) What are the policies and procedures regulating joining the Jewish people (as best we can determine from the extant records)?

BIBLICAL PERIOD

Patriarchal Period

We begin our discussion with the biblical period, which itself spans approximately 1,500 years. The issue of who absorbs/assimilates whom is evident in the earliest biblical records dealing with marriages in the patriarchal period. The patriarchs and matriarchs were deeply involved with their children's marriage choices. Living in the land of Canaan, they feared that their children would intermarry with the Canaanites and that such marriages would spell the spiritual demise of the nascent Hebrew faith. The Canaanites, being more numerous, would easily assimilate the patriarchal family through such marriages. Thus, Abraham, the first Jew, instructs his servant Eliezer, "You will not take a wife for my son from the daughters of the Canaanites among whom I live, but you will go to the land of my birth and to my own kinfolk and get a wife for my son Isaac" (Genesis 24:3–4). Abraham preferred that his son's wife come from a distant land so that there would be a lesser likelihood of his son's being assimilated by his wife's kindred. The wife's family, removed from their daughter, would not be able to exert a religious influence on the newlyweds, which would be the case if the wife came from one of the neighboring tribes. Had Abraham been mainly concerned that Isaac marry only within his own family, the following dialogue between Abraham and his servant Eliezer would not have been necessary. Eliezer says to Abraham, "What if the woman does not want to come with me to this land, must I take your son back to the land from which you came?" Abraham replies, "On no account should you take my son back there" (Genesis 24:5–6). The issue is not only whom Isaac was going to marry but also where and under what influence he would live. What Abraham feared most was the removal of his son to a distant land where he would come under the influence of a different faith. A wife of Isaac coming from an idolatrous background must not reside near her family who would encourage the idolatry.

Similarly the patriarch Isaac blessed Jacob and charged him, "You shall not marry one of the Canaanite women. Arise, go to Paddan-aram to the house of Bethuel your mother's father, and there choose a wife for yourself from among the daughters of Laban your mother's brother" (Genesis 28:1–2). Jacob marries Rachael and Leah and, despite his fear of his brother Esau, he sees the need to return home, for otherwise his family would be assimilated by Rachael's and Leah's relatives.

The concern in the patriarchal period was understandable. Monotheism was a new religious concept, and there was a justifiable fear that the new faith would be strangled in its infancy by the prevailing idolatrous neighboring civilization. Although Abraham's kin residing in Mesopotamia were also idolators, as we learn from the narrative of Rachael stealing her father's idols (Genesis 31:8–35), nevertheless, since these wives would be taken from their parental environment, they would be distanced from the influence of their family and their native faith. When Esau, the other son of Isaac, marries a nearby Hittite woman not from the family we are told, "and they [the Hittite women] were a source of bitterness to Isaac and Rebecca" (Genesis 26:35). The implied rule for the survival of monotheism in the patriarchal period was to fend off the neighboring culture by keeping children and spouses close to home and above all to avoid marriages with the offspring of nearby tribes.

The patriarchal period can be summed up in the words spoken by Abraham in describing his status: "I am a resident alien among you . . ." (Genesis 23:4). The patriarchs lived among idolators and in order to transmit their new faith to future generations, they set boundaries particularly in marriages between themselves and others lest their children would be assimilated by their neighbors. At this point of development, religious and ethnic (peoplehood, cultural) aspects were congruous, and marriage was the procedure by which one "entered the family" and thereby the religion.

Early Israelite Period

The patriarchal concern was carried over into the premonarchal period when the Israelite tribes reached the promised land after the Exodus from Egypt. The biblical books of Joshua and Judges record constant battles with the neighboring tribes in the land of Canaan, and deep concern about intermarriage was evident. The Bible establishes an outright prohibition of intermarriage with the Canaanites in the early Israelite period: "You must not marry them; you must not give a daughter of yours to a son of theirs nor take a daughter of theirs for a son of yours, for this would turn away your children from following me to serving others gods" (Deuteronomy 7:3–4). Those people lived in close proximity to the Israelites, and the possibility of assimilation to their culture was real. The term *Canaanite* applied to all seven nations living in the land of Canaan in close proximity to the Israelites. Other biblical prohibitions against mixed marriages directed against the Ammonites, Moabites, and Egyptians had to do with historical memories of antagonistic relationships and not the concern about absorption/assimilation. Intermarriages with non-Israelite individuals who came from other lands but lived in Canaan were not prohibited. For example, the Bible permits a soldier to marry his captive. Here, though, is described a separation ritual, for the captive woman had to shave her head, cut her nails, and for a month mourn her parents who were to be considered dead (Deuteronomy 21:10–14). As the noted biblical scholar Yehezkel Kaufmann points out,

> In biblical days the prohibition of mixed marriages was directed at specific nations, but otherwise intermarriage was permitted. Ammonites and Moabites are excluded for historical reasons (Deuteronomy 23:4). Egypt, on the other hand, is favored for historical reasons (Deuteronomy 23:8–9). . . . The sources speak continually of mixtures between Israel and the nations. . . . The rule was that the third generation [of Egyptians and Edomites] who settled in Israel was permitted to join the community of "YAHWEH" and was considered Israelite (Deuteronomy 23:8) (1960, p. 308).

There is no term for proselyte (convert) in the Bible. The original denotation of *ger* in the Bible means simply a stranger. The identification of the term *ger* (*gioret,* the feminine term) as proselyte is found much later in rabbinic, medieval, and modern literature.

The non-Israelite, the *ger,* who married an Israelite was evidently not asked to go through a conversion ceremony as an abandonment of one faith or people in favor of another faith or way of life. The Bible indicates a naturalization process was accepted rather than a specific symbolic act of commitment to a faith. The concept of *ger* is treated twenty-seven times in the Pentateuch and nowhere is an obstacle placed on a *ger* marrying an Israelite. The underlying rule is "one law to the stranger and homeborn in your midst" (Numbers 15:15). There are a few distinctions between a *ger* and a homeborn, but marriage was not one of them. The main differences were religious, relating to sacrifical acts for the *ger.* For example, the *ger* was not obligated to follow the dietary laws and, thus, a nonkosher animal or carcass could be sold to him or her. In addition, during the Commonwealth period, the *ger* could not become king, very much like the provision of the Constitution of the United States that the office of president is to be filled by a native born citizen. Otherwise impediments were not placed upon a *ger.* He or she was permitted to marry an Israelite.

Historical research of that period also has not produced definitive evidence that circumcision of the male, a time-hallowed practice among Jews dating back to the time of Abraham and universally practiced today, was required of the *ger* who married a Jew. Abraham was commanded: "When they are eight days old, all your male children must be circumcised, generation after generation of them, no matter whether they be born within your household or bought with your money" (Genesis 17:2–13). This command would logically imply that in joining a Jewish household a non-Israelite would be required to undergo circumcision. However, it can also be maintained that the term "bought with your money" is directed specifically to servants who were considered the property of their masters and, hence, the covenantal requirements including circumcision also applied to them. Likewise, circumcision is mentioned for a *ger* living in Canaan who wished to partake of the Paschal sacrifice. The eating of such a sacrifice is also indicative of a covenantal relationship between the Jewish people and God. To enter into the covenant, one had to be fully Jewish, and circumcision was mandated. But nowhere, except for the aforementioned covenantal reasons, is circumcision mandated. In that period marriage was not a covenantal rite. Here may be our first indication of the separation of religious from ethnic-kin roles. Higher standards apply for full religious participation than for mere family relationships.

The biblical incident of Dinah and Shechem does not refute the above statement. Dinah was violated by Shechem, the son of Hamor (Genesis 34:1–31). Shechem, a heathen, then wished to marry the daughter of Jacob whom he had raped. He is advised by Jacob's sons that he and his entire tribe would have to undergo circumcision. The biblical text suggests that this ad hoc requirement was made due to the concern of Jacob's family over Shechem's father's invitation to assimilate: "Intermarry with us; give your daughters to us, take our daughters for yourselves, *and you will dwell among us*" (our emphasis) (Genesis 34:9). It seems from the text that the situation was a case of a Jewish family in danger of being assimilated by the dominant population; they were a small familial group surrounded by large powerful tribes. Therefore, a strict requirement was added for intermarriage.[2]

As the tribes gradually settled down in the land, they found themselves frequently involved in battles with neighboring kingdoms. Initially, the were satisfied to have temporary military and organizational leadership provided by so-called judges, with priests providing religious leadership. Eventually, though, they felt the

---

2. The subsequent killing of the Shechemites after the circumcisions raises some doubt as to whether the circumcisions were requested to facilitate intermarriage, to dissuade Shechem because of the serious requirement, or to weaken the Shechemites so they could more easily be slaughtered.

need for a more centralized ruling structure, and against the wishes of God as conveyed by Samuel, a prophet-priest, demanded a king. With the crowning of Saul, the first Jewish Commonwealth was established about 1000 BCE.[3] As a sovereign people, the Israelites' fear of foreign influences was lessened and a hospitable attitude toward marriage with the stranger emerged. King Solomon, in order to forge alliances with the surrounding people, married many gentile wives, and not even the voices of the prophets were raised against him. For the next 600 years, the prophets warned against worship of foreign gods but did not call for a ban on intermarriage. In 722 BCE, when the northern ten tribes were taken captive by the Assyrians, prophets in the remaining kingdom of Judea continually warned against social injustice and falling away from God's laws but did not add restrictions to the role of the *ger*. This lenient state of affairs lasted until the destruction of the First Commonwealth by the Babylonians in 586 BCE.

In sum, in this postpatriarchal period when the Israelites were in control of their land and had their own government, they were allowed to intermarry with any but their historical enemies without restrictions. Apparently, the Israelites were sufficiently confident that the stranger would be integrated into the dominant life of the people and believed that the danger of their sons and daughters following the way of the heathens because of intermarriage was nonexistent.

The rite of circumcision is not mentioned in the Bible as a requirement for marriage. To be sure, it may also be argued that the rite was such a hallowed practice that silence may suggest that it was taken for granted that a *ger* underwent circumcision if he married a Jew. However, it can be stated with a degree of certainty that no formal ceremony of conversion was mandated in that phase of Jewish history.

Thus, we see that the patriarchal period and the early Israelite period illustrate that when the faith of the community is threatened by outside forces, severe restrictions are placed on intermarriage, and when the community sees no threat, intermarriage restrictions are not promulgated. During those periods, there were no standardized procedures for conversion rites, since one was accepted into the Jewish community through association and not conversion. No term

---

3. BCE is the scholarly and Jewish designation, Before the Common Era, for the time period some Christians call BC.

for proselyte is found in the Bible, and circumcision is mandated for full religious participation but not for marriage. The distinction of circumcision for religious but not for marital participation marks the beginning of separation of ethnic from religious concerns, which had not been distinguished in the patriarchial period.

End of the Biblical Period

At the close of the First Commonwealth when the Temple was destroyed in 586 BCE by the Babylonian Empire, the open attitude toward the stranger that prevailed in the postpatriarchal times was no longer acceptable to all authorities. With the loss of Jewish sovereignty and a large segment of the people in captivity, mixed marriages became a major concern. "Who would absorb/assimilate whom" was back on the Jewish agenda. In 536 BCE, Ezra and Nehemiah were authorized by Cyrus the Great of Persia, who had defeated the Babylonians, to rebuild the Temple and to establish a second Jewish Commonwealth. When those leaders returned from exile they found chaotic conditions in Jerusalem. The local population was depleted and demoralized. The historian Salo Baron estimates that "fully a third of the pre-war population of Judea was forcibly removed by the conqueror; the Jews, bereft of leadership, began to intermarry in great numbers and the popular religion of Canaan asserted itself" (1952, p. 85). Those intermarriages resulted in the emergence of a group of people known as the Samaritans. They consisted of foreign colonists and the descendents of the Israelites who escaped the destruction of the Northern Kingdom of Israel at the hands of the Assyrians in 722 BCE. Their religion was a mixture of Judaism and idolatry. When the Samaritans offered assistance in rebuilding the Temple, Ezra and Nehemiah feared their influence on the returnees and, also fearing that the future survival of Judaism was at stake, took drastic measures in order to eliminate alien influences. Ezra and Nehemiah proscribed marriages with the Samaritans. "We will not give our daughters to the peoples of the land or take their daughters for our sons" (Nehemiah 10:30). In the book of Ezra, we find an even harsher statement. In the renewal of the covenant between the people of Israel and God, Ezra insisted that the men who had intermarried had to break up their marriages and families. "Now, therefore let us make a covenant with our God to put away all foreign wives and the children born to them" (Ezra 10:3). Marriage was no longer to be viewed as a personal arrangement between families but was to be part of a covental (religious) relationship with God and, therefore, subject to strict controls.

The self-confident attitude toward the *ger* that we find during the First Commonwealth abated during the days of the second Temple, 536 BCE to 70 CE. Throughout most of the period of the Second Commonwealth, Israel was subservient to foreign rulers and never recovered the sense of confidence that marked its predecessor, the kingdom established by the House of David. The fear of being assimilated that prevailed in Judea because of its internal weakness was also due to the changed position of the Jew in the ancient world. Judea was no longer the only center of Jewish life. The Jews who returned with Ezra and Nehemiah to the land of Judea were impoverished while the most affluent ones continued to live in Babylonia and developed a creative community. As Persia gave way to Greece and the armies of Alexander the Great conquered the Near East, new opportunities for commerce developed. Jewish merchants began to travel great distances, and those who settled outside of Judea formed substantial diasporas. Centers of Jewish life sprang up in Egypt, Rome, Syria, and other far-flung communities. Jews interacted with gentiles, and both exerted influences on each other. Many Jews were attracted to Hellenism, and many gentiles were attracted to Judaism, which up to that time had been relatively unknown outside of Judea. The danger of foreign influences became more acute, and a serious concern about marriage outside the faith and people followed. Consequently, the beginning of formal conversion to Judaism emerged, leading to the requirement of circumcision for males.[4]

A famous case of circumcision for the purpose of conversion is recorded in the writings of Josephus, a Jewish historian in the period of the Second Commonwealth. Josephus relates the story of the conversion of Queen Helena and her son, Izates of Adiabene, a kingdom in the upper Tigris region. Helena converted first. Following the queen's conversion, her son, Izates, who came under the influence of a Jewish merchant, Ananias, decided to follow his mother's example. When Eleazar, a Galilean Jew, heard about the conversion, he urged Izates to undergo circumcision despite the fact

---

4. We are aware of the forced Idomite conversions during the period of the Maccabees; however, many scholars maintain that those conversions were for political rather than religious or ethnic reasons. Therefore, we have not used this event as an example.

that Helena and Ananias did not consider it necessary to do so. Eleazar, however, was insistent. His plea was that the lack of circumcision would be "the greatest offense against the law and thereby against God" (*Antiquties* 20:34 ff).

The Adiabene tale is an important illustration of a community increasingly becoming wary about those eager to join it. On one hand, the fact that others wished to join the Jewish ranks was a source of satisfaction to the Jew; but, on the other hand, there were those who were concerned lest a large number of joiners would lead to increased foreign influences and a distortion of historic Judaism. One way to resolve the issue was to insist on stringent requirements for admission into the fold. The biblical concept of the *ger,* the stranger living in the land of Israel, was now broadened to include the one who is a *ger,* a stranger who never set foot in Judea. For that *ger* the requirement of circumcision was called for by some of the rabbis. We also find that at the end of the Second Commonwealth, new terms were used in addition to that of *ger.* In the late books of the Bible (see, for example, Esther 8:1), we find the word *mityahadim,* gentiles becoming Jewish. In Malachai, another late book in the Bible, a gentile who accepted part but not the totality of Judaism was no longer called a *ger* but a "fearer of the Lord."

Throughout the Second Commonwealth period, there was an ambivalence in the approach to gentiles who wished to join the Jewish people. While Ezra and Nehemiah, as previously stated, were exclusionary in their approach, there were others at that time who were concerned that exclusion would lead to the insulation of the Jewish community. Thus, the book of Ruth, which according to many modern Bible scholars originated during the period, is understood as a polemic against the ban on intermarriage issued by Ezra and Nehemiah. Ruth, in addition to being a gentile, is also a Moabite whom Scripture categorically prohibits from entering *Khal Adonai,* the congregation of Israel, until the tenth generation. The widow Ruth, who had lived with her Jewish husband outside the land of Israel, clings to her mother-in-law, Naomi, and pleads to be allowed to return with Naomi to the land of Israel. Ruth's words to Naomi, "Entreat me not to leave you and to return from following after you; for where you go I will go, where you lodge I will lodge, your people will be my people, and your God my God" (Ruth 1:16), have become symbolic of proselytes who accept Judaism enthusiastically. Ruth follows Naomi back to the land of Israel, marries a Jewish man, and, tradition has it, became the great-grandmother of the revered King

David. No conversion ceremony is recorded for Ruth. Ruth is the Jew by choice par excellence. It is only at a later date, as we shall see, that the rabbis interpreted the story of Ruth in such a manner that Ruth's words become criteria for conversion.

The author of Ruth, obviously, welcomed the gentile and, if it is a polemic against Ezra and Nehemiah, as many scholars believe, the book's message is that in the land of Israel the gentile will eventually be absorbed and, therefore, mixed marriages pose no threat to the community.

In summary, we see that the exile in 586 BCE shook the confidence of the Jews in their ability to survive on the basis of nationalism alone. Ezra and Nehemiah, architects of the Second Commonwealth, upon their return from Babylonian exile feared the syncretization of the Jewish faith taking place in the land of Israel and the influences emanating from the growing diasporas. They demanded of Jews purity of faith and required that marriages be consecrated only between born Jews. The Second Commonwealth that they established never had the same measure of sovereignty as the First Commonwealth. At its inception it was ruled by the Persian Empire, later the Jews became dependent on the good will of Alexander the Great, and during the Maccabean era, Hellenism, the Greek influence on the ancient world, weakened the loyalty of the Jewish community toward their ancestral faith. In the latter part of the biblical period, in contrast to its earlier period, the convenantal aspects of Judaism rather than its familial or national aspects begin to emerge. The book of Ruth is probably a polemic against this trend.

To review the information about proselytes for the entire biblical period, three attitudes can be discerned. In the patriarchal tales we are told of a small familial group dedicated to monotheism, determined to transmit their religion to their children. Fearful of outside influences, they hoped that their children would marry only within their extended family, live close to them, and be influenced by their example. Marriages with nearby strangers were discouraged. As the family tribes increased, they forged themselves into a kingdom, with a land of their own, being ruled by judges and then by kings and having a central religious sanctuary. As a sovereign people, they were unafraid to marry a stranger living in their midst who accepted monotheism. They were confident that the *ger* would eventually be absorbed into the life of the people. In the latter part of the biblical period, which was a time of turmoil for the Commonwealth with its future threatened by powerful empires, the religious leadership began to emphasize the covenantal aspects of the religion and demand a purity of faith in order to stave off religious syncretism.

TALMUDIC PERIOD

Problems for the Jewish people intensified with the destruction of the second Temple in the year 70 CE by the Romans and the crushing defeat of the Bar Kochba rebellion in 135 CE, which put an end to the Jewish Commonwealth. The land and the temple that united the people in the past were gone and could no longer serve as a unifying force. Jews who lived in the various diasporas such as Babylonia, Egypt, or Rome continued to be exposed to foreign social and intellectual ideas by their neighbors. In addition, Christianity, which also professed monotheism, was becoming a power. The Talmud, a unique work containing discussions among the rabbis over a period of six centuries, 100 BCE to 500 CE, dealt with these enormous problems. The discussions gave rise to what is known today as rabbinic Judaism. The Talmud is the authoritative guide even today and is important for our discussion of proselytism. In the Talmud, rabbis charted a new course for the entrance of a gentile into the Jewish community. These events affected attitudes toward proselytism. The Talmud no longer defined a *ger* as one who lived in a sovereign Jewish state who could be absorbed in the community but as one who enters into a covenantal community. The *ger,* having no option for citizenship, had to undergo a formal conversion ritual that initiated him or her into a religious covenantal community. The proselyte was required to appear before three Jews who constitute a *bet din,* a court of Jewish law, and they were to address him or her as follows:

> "What reason have you for desiring to become a proselyte; do you not know that Israel at the present time is persecuted and oppressed, despised, harassed, and overcome by affliction?" If he replies, "I know and yet am unworthy," he is accepted forthwith and is given instruction in some minor and major commandments (*Yebamot* 24b).

The male proselyte is to undergo circumcision and both the female and the male are required to immerse themselves in a *mikvah,* a ritual bath. In making religious decisions, the rabbis try to find rationale in the biblical texts for their innovations; therefore, they found precedents for formal conversion in the Torah. Since the first Jew, Abraham, underwent circumcision as a sign of a *brit,* a covenant, the proselyte, in rabbinic teaching, likewise is "a new born babe" and through circumcision becomes the spiritual child of Abraham to be absorbed into the covenantal community founded by the patriarch.

In addition, the immersion of proselytes in water is also a covenantal rite derived from a biblical interpretation of Israel's covenant with God at Mount Sinai. They were commanded through Moses, "go to the people, sanctify them today and tomorrow, and let them wash their garments" (Exodus 19:10). The rabbis adduce from these biblical verses that if one was to wash one's garments for sanctification, surely one was to wash oneself. (See commentary on the verse by Hertz, 1938, p. 292.) And since the covenant of the past represented a change of status, a cleansing of oneself from past beliefs, and a new start, the proselyte now also had to undergo these rituals.

The conversion ceremony represents a new mind-set toward the gentile world. One could no longer be naturally absorbed within the community. A proselyte had to undergo religious ritual requirements if he or she wished to be a Jew and could no longer marry a Jew unless all the requirements for conversion were first met. A conversion ritual constituted a radical departure from biblical days when a *ger* living in Judea was required only to observe ethical principles known as the seven Noahide laws. The *ger* in the Talmud is required to observe all the commandments even as a born Jewish son or daughter is commanded. The biblical concept of *ger* as a resident alien ceases to exist in the Talmudic era and is replaced by the concept of the *ger tzedek,* the righteous proselyte.

As a result of these strict requirements there arose the problem of large numbers of gentiles who were attracted to Judaism but who were not ready to fulfill the ritual requirements imposed by the religious authorities. Their absorption into the Jewish community was vigorously debated. Could a covenantal community maintain its character if a large number of would-be proselytes brought up with alien beliefs were absorbed, or would they eventually dilute the covenant? Some religious authorities maintained that proselytes and potential proselytes were not to be encouraged and that the rules of admission should be stringent, while others wished to remove as many obstacles as possible, maintaining that Judaism is a universal religion and gentiles should be encouraged to come "under the wings of God." The debate was not a theoretical discussion for Jewish learning but had immediate ramifications. The historian Josephus (38–100 CE), who lived during the time of the collapse of the Jewish state and the ascendancy of the diaspora, described the vast appeal that Judaism had for the gentile:

> The masses have long since shown a keen desire to adopt our religious observances, and there is not one city, Greek or barbarian, nor a single nation to which our custom of abstaining from work on the seventh day has not spread and where fasts and the lighting of lamps and many other prohibitions in matter of food is not observed (as cited by Baron, 1952, pp. 173–174).

What was to be the attitude toward those who adhered to many Jewish practices but had reservations about a total acceptance of the covenantal requirements? Were they to be treated as outsiders or were they to be accepted in some form? Should Jews maintain a mission to the outside world? These were some of the questions that agitated rabbinic thought. There is no definitive evidence in Jewish sources that Jews engaged in missionary activities as the Christian New Testament claims, "Woe to you, scribes and Pharisees, you hypocrites for you travel over sea and land to make one proselyte and, when you have him, you make him twice as fit for hell as you are" (Matthew 23:15). However, missionizing can be accomplished by exemplary living, and Jews who settled in all parts of the ancient world practicing Judaism drew many gentiles to their belief by example. George Foote Moore, in his monumental work *Judaism in the First Centuries of the Christian Era*, writes,

> The belief in the future universality of the true religion . . . led to efforts to convert the gentiles to worship the one true God . . . and made Judaism the first missionary religion of the Mediterranean world. . . . The phrase must, however, be understood with a difference. The Jews did not send out missionaries . . . to proselytize among the heathen. They were themselves settled by the thousands in all the great centers and in innumerable smaller cities. . . . Their religious influences were exerted chiefly through synagogues . . . which were open to all whom interest and curiosity drew to their service (1927, pp. 323–326).

The talmudic passages bearing on proselytism seem to confirm the fact that the rabbis were keen on spreading their faith to the gentile communities, and many spoke with great enthusiasm regarding converts. Not only were they open to proselytism, but some would accept proselytes without any prior condition. Passages in the Talmud, particularly statements from Hillel the Elder (end of first century BCE to beginning of first century CE), illustrate this willingness to share Judaism with gentiles.

Hillel would accept proselytes who refused to adhere to rabbinic teaching by only accepting the written law, namely the Torah, but not the oral law. A native Jew who would utter such sentiments would have been labeled a heretic. Nevertheless, Hillel was favorably disposed to such proselytes. The Talmud records that a certain heathen once came before Shammai and asked him, "How many Torahs have you?"

"Two," he replied, "the Written Torah and the Oral Torah."
"I believe you with respect to the Written but not with respect to the Oral Torah. Make me a proselyte on condition that you teach me the Written Torah (only)."
(But) he scolded him and repulsed him with anger. When he went before Hillel, he accepted him as a proselyte (*Shabbat* 31a).

The significance in this passage is that Hillel the Elder encouraged the heathen to join the covenantal community. Of course, the Talmud states that Hillel eventually convinced the proselyte to study and to accept the oral law as well, but the text also reveals the attitude of Hillel that initially it is incumbent on rabbis not to discourage gentiles who are exploring the possibility of joining the Jewish community. The same Hillel also would encourage a prospective proselyte to join the Jewish community even though he asked to be converted to Judaism for the sake of becoming a high priest (*Shabbat* 31a). To Hillel, conversion was the *beginning* of a relationship of Jewish religious practice, not the end.

Other authorities like Hillel wished to eliminate as many barriers as possible in order to encourage proselytism. Even as late as the second century CE, mandatory circumcision and use of the *mikvah* for converts became a subject of debate between Rabbi Eliezer and Rabbi Joshua. According to Rabbi Eliezer, if the candidate was circumcised but had not been immersed in the *mikvah* water, he was a "bona fide" proselyte. According to Rabbi Joshua, if he performed the proper immersion ablution but was not circumcised, he was a proper proselyte (*Yebamot* 46a). Each rabbi validated his statement with quotations from Scripture, but could we not speculate that, even as late as the second century, there were rabbis who maintained that neither circumcision nor immersion were the sine qua non for conversion? Is it possible to reason that there were rabbis who not only begrudgingly accepted converts but who encouraged proselytism by removing many of the ritualistic requirements that at times served as an impediment?

Scattered throughout the Talmud one finds an openness toward proselytism. "The Holy One, Blessed be He, exiled Israel among the nations only in order to increase proselytes" (*Pesachim* 87b). A benediction formulated in talmudic times that to this day is recited daily at services includes a prayer in praise of the proselyte. "Toward the righteous and pious, toward the elders of Thy people, the House of Israel, toward the proselytes of righteousness, and toward us also, may Thy tender mercies be stirred, O Lord our God" (*Tosefta Berakhot* 3:25). Rabbis taught that the proselyte should be fully accepted by Jews. "He who perverts justice against a proselyte is deemed as though he has turned against God Himself" (*Hagigah* 5a). No slur was permitted against a Jew whose parents were converts. "You must not reproach a descendent of proselytes with his former ancestry" (*Mishnah Baba Mezia* 4:10). Rabbi Simon b. Lakish, a third century Palestinian scholar, idealized the convert. "The proselyte is more beloved unto God than the multitudes at Sinai, for this one accepted the Kingdom of Heaven without rumble and thunder" (Braude, 1940, p. 25).

Talmudic legends abound with biblical personalities who obviously were gentiles, but in the legends they appear as proselytes. Conversion was ascribed to Bithia, the daughter of Pharaoh who saved Moses; Jethro, the father-in-law of Moses; and Rehab, who helped Joshua capture Jericho and who became an ancestor of the prophet Jeremiah (Braude, 1940, p. 36). In rabbinic tradition proselytes, or sons of proselytes, are some of the most distinguished rabbis; for example, Shemiah, the head of the Sanhedrin (Jewish supreme court) in the fifth century BCE and his colleague Avtalyon; Aquilla, the translator of the Bible into Greek; Rabbi Meir, whose legal opinions are said to be the basis for the *Mishnah;* and Rabbi Akiba, a scholar and martyred patriot of the second century CE (*Sanhedrin* 96b).

Laudatory statements and sentiments about converts were by no means unanimous. There were rabbis who questioned whether a powerless people suffering the loss of Jewish sovereignty could absorb gentiles in great numbers or whether Judaism would be syncretized by the gentile world unless it maintained its purity. The Talmud thus records both laudatory and unfriendly statements, but at no time is conversion ruled out. Often we read that the same rabbi who made an unfriendly statement acknowledged in another case that a true proselyte was to be accepted without any reservations. Thus, Rabbi Eliezer ben Hyrcanus who said, "It is because the proselyte's temper is bad that scripture warns him in many places" also said, "when a man comes to you wishing to convert to Judaism as long as he comes in the name of God, for the sake of heaven, do thou likewise befriend him and do not repel him" (*Mekhilta Amalek* 3, cited by Braude, 1940, p. 40). Rabbi Hiyya said, "Put no confidence in a proselyte until the twenty-fourth generation for he holds onto his leaven," yet the same Rabbi Hiyya said "when a proselyte accepts the yoke of heaven in love and fear and is converted for the sake of heaven . . . God loves the proselyte" (cited by Braude, 1940, p. 41).

No uniform attitude toward the convert is found in the period of the Talmud. The Talmud records a collection of individual opinions, some in praise of converts, others in judgment. We can only speculate that much had to do with the respective rabbi's experiences with gentiles. Rabbi Helbo, a third century rabbi who lived during a repressive period under the Roman Empire, probably expressed his opinion based on his personal experience when he said, "converts are as obnoxious to Israel as leprosy" (*Yebamot* 47:b). It is noteworthy that the commentary *Tosafot* (*Yebamot* 42b) considers this statement to be complementary because Rabbi Helbo also states, "converts are more careful regarding the commandments than other Jews, hence the difficulty Israel has in emulating them." On the other hand, Rav, who lived in the first century CE in Babylonia under peaceful conditions, gladly welcomed converts. "Whoever comes to be converted should be accepted. Do not inquire into motives of would-be converts. We may assume that they come for the sake of heaven."

The ambivalence in the talmudic period was resolved by establishing a uniform practice for conversion. If one wished to join the covenantal community, a male had to undergo circumcision and immersion and a female immersion. The convert was obligated to accept the teachings of *halachic* Judaism. A conversion ceremony was to take place in the presence of a *bet din,* a court of Jewish law consisting of three knowledgeable Jews. This format was accepted only after much debate.

Since the talmudic authorities authenticated their decrees by tracing their decisions to earlier sources, particularly the Bible, how were they now to justify the revered biblical personalities who married gentiles without any conversion, such as Joseph who married Asenath, an Egyptian daughter of a priest; Moses who married Zipporah, a daughter of a Midianite priest; and Boaz who married Ruth, a Moabite? The rabbis reinterpreted the ancient texts, reading into them the ceremony of conversion. One such example is in the interpretation given to the story of Ruth.

Kind David traced his ancestry to Ruth, yet we find no evidence of conversion of this Moabite woman in the book of Ruth. To the talmudic rabbis, this was unthinkable. Therefore, a legend based on the biblical story of Ruth was used to solve the dilemma for them.

According to the *Midrash,* since Ruth's decision to return to Israel could not be shaken, her mother-in-law, Naomi, in compliance with Jewish law that a prospective convert must at first be discouraged, warns her that Israelites must keep the Sabbath and feast days, to which Ruth answered, "where you go, I will go." (According to *Yebamot* 47a, the attention of the prospective convert must be directed to these ceremonial laws.) "Where you lodge, I will lodge" shows Ruth's acceptance of the restriction on a female being alone with a male who is not her husband. Naomi further says to Ruth, "We have one Torah, one God, one law, one command, the Eternal is one." Ruth answers, "Thy people shall be my people [accepting the 613 commandments incumbent on Jews] and thy God my God." "By whatever means you die, I will die" shows Ruth's understanding of the four forms of capital punishment used by the Jewish court—stoning, burning, decapitation, and strangulation. "And there I will be buried" demonstrates Ruth's acceptance of the rules of burial. "And she [Naomi] ceased speaking to her [Ruth]" indicates that Naomi's task was to present Ruth with some information on major laws and punishments, attempt to dissuade her from undertaking the obligations of a Jew, but not to overburden or cross-examine her too closely. When Ruth comes to Judea, despite her meeting the requirements for conversion, her brother-in-law refuses to marry her. According to the rabbinic interpretation of this story, which seems to sanction behavior that is against a direct biblical statement, Boaz was unaware that the law forbade only a Moabite *male* from entering *Khal Adonai;* a Moabite woman was permitted to do so. Becoming aware of the law, Boaz marries her (Ginzberg, 1941, pp. 32–34).

In summary, the talmudic period saw a restructuring of Judaism. The survival of the faith was threatened by the loss of statehood, dispersion, increased contacts with the gentile world, and the absence of a central authority. To fill the vacuum left by those developments, the emphasis shifted to a strengthening of the covenantal relationships between God and Israel. By entering that relationship, it was hoped that the proselyte would be able to overcome the pressures of the outside world and be totally absorbed into the Jewish community. A formal conversion procedure was designed to focus on that covenantal relationship. Thus, such requirements as circumcision, immersion in the *mikvah,* and acceptance of the commandments became part of normative Judaism. The *ger tzedek,* the righteous proselyte, meeting these requirements would in fact be a source of strength to the covenantal community.

The talmudic period also had to confront another challenge vis-à-vis the gentile world. Prior to the rise of Christianity, the issue seemed to have been how to insulate Judaism from outside influences and how to make certain that the convert knowlingly accepted the covenant between God and the Jewish people. With the rise of Christianity, new realities emerged that in fact if not in theory resulted in a moratorium on conversion to Judaism.

Much of the world population was ready for a change from pagan polytheism to ethical monotheism, but, whereas Judaism in the past attracted gentiles, now the new faith, Christianity, won the hearts and minds of the pagan world. The stringent talmudic requirements, particularly circumcision for conversion even for adult males, served as a source of discouragement. The gentile could now choose Christianity with fewer religious requirements as the road to monotheism, and the popularity of Judaism began to diminish. Paul found a ready-made audience for his missionary work. The book of Acts describes Paul as preaching in the synagogue of Antioch "to Jews and you that fear God." The message inspired gentiles more than those who were born Jews. Paul is portrayed as being annoyed with the Jews who doubted his message. "It was necessary that the word of God should first have been spoken to you [Jews], but since you put it from you and judge yourself unworthy of everlasting life, we turn to the gentiles" (Acts 13:46). His message was directed to gentiles who could now leave their former faith. Without accepting Judaism, they could transfer from paganism to Christianity. In addition, circumcision that was required by talmudic law was not mandated by Christianity. "In Christ Jesus neither circumcision nor uncircumcision is of any avail but [only] faith working through love" (Galatians 5:l6). The gentile seeking a new faith, attending the synagogue, being attracted to Judaism, but not being fully converted heard a new message that offered monotheism without the strictness of the talmudic laws.

POST–TALMUDIC PERIOD

As Christianity established itself in the world, the number of conversions to Judaism was greatly limited. Not only because Christianity won the hearts and minds of the pagan world, but also because in the fourth century CE, when Christianity became the official faith of the Roman Empire, conversion to Judaism was forbidden on pain of death. That edict for capital punishment promulgated in 315 CE was later expanded in 403 CE to apply not only to the Christian convert but also to members of the Jewish court who accepted a gentile as a convert. As a result, from the days of Constantine until the breaching of the ghetto walls at the end of the eighteenth century, proselytism to Judaism became a rare phenomenon.

It is noteworthy that even in the early Christian period when the transfer from one religion to another was considered a capital offense, there were courageous souls who joined the Jewish community and managed to find an equally courageous accepting *bet din.* The proselyte fearing for his life had to hide and to roam from one country to another as a fugitive from "justice." This was the fate of the Archibishop Andreas, chief priest of the province of Bari (now in southeast Italy), who had to flee to Egypt to save himself. In 1102 a Norman proselyte, Obadiah, a first-year student in the priesthood greatly influenced by Andreas, wrote pamphlets calling upon Christians to return to the religion of Israel, and, after the Christian authorities imprisoned him, he succeeded in escaping to Baghdad. Obadiah visited Jewish communities in Syria, Palestine, and Egypt, was befriended by the head of the Baghdad academy, and lived in his home for some time (*Encyclopedia Judaica,* 1977, p. 1187).

One should not think that the former Archbishop Andreas and Norman, the proselyte, found a haven in the Moslem part of the world because Moslems were more tolerant of proselytism than Christians; they were not. Christian converts to Judaism were safe in Islamic countries because it was not against the Islamic faith for a Christian to become a Jew; however, Islam forbade conversion from Islam either to Judaism or to Christianity. A series of discriminatory regulations were promulgated during the Caliphate of Omar (634–644 CE) making pariahs of Jews and Christians. Moslems were bidden to convert non-Moslems but did not object if Jews converted Christians to Judaism.

That proselytism occurred in the Middle Ages we see from the writings of Judah Halevi (1086–1145 CE). The historian Graetz (1949) reflected the esteem that Jews bore Halevi: "to describe him fully, one would have to borrow from poetry and her richest colors and her sweetest song." One of the greatest philosophical Jewish writings, known as the *Sefer-ha-Kuzari,* written by Judah Halevi, is based on an episode in Jewish history in the year 740 CE. It describes the conversion of the Khazars, a Tartar nation located on the western banks of the Caspian Sea between the Don and the Volga.

A dialogue takes place in which a Christian, a Moslem, an Aristotelian, and a Jew appear before Budan, king of the Khazars. The king listens to the arguments presented but is particularly impressed with the Jewish representative Hver as he expounds from Judaism on philosophy, liturgy, history, and concepts of God, Messiah, and the Holy Land. When the Khazar monarch alludes to the degraded condition of the Jew, Hver rejoins,

> Do not believe that I, though agreeing with thee, admit that we are dead. We still hold connection with the Divine influence through the laws which He has placed in us as a link between us and Him. . . . We are not like the dead but rather like a sick and attenuated person who has been given up by the physicians, but yet hopes for a miracle or an extraordinary recovery (Minkin, 1963, p. 124).

The king accepts the Jewish religion both for himself and for his people. The Jewish kingdom lasted until 969 CE when it suffered its ultimate defeat by the Duke of Kiev.

The tale of the conversion of the Khazars is significant for our study on two counts. First, the setting is in a land that was free from Christian and Moslem intolerance. In the absence of pressure from Christianity and Islam, Judaism had an opportunity to present its case and in a free contest could prevail. Second, the fact that in the Middle Ages Judah Halevi chose the episode of conversion of the Khazars as a vehicle for expounding Judaism shows that the biblical eschatological hope for the ultimate conversion of humanity to Judaism was still very much alive in the hearts of Jews. It is noteworthy that little is found in Jewish medieval writings about the Khazar kingdom even though the *Sefer-ha-Kuzari* was studied diligently as a philosophical text of Judaism. Could it be that living in Christian or Moslem lands, Jews avoided that part of their history for fear that the tale about conversion to Judaism would not be looked upon with favor by the governments of those countries?

Another medieval figure, Maimonides (1135–1204 CE), widely described as the greatest rabbi since the days of Moses, likewise left no doubt about his attitude toward proselytism. Obadiah, a convert to Judaism, addressed a question to Maimonides. In the daily prayers a Jew recites "Our God and God of our Fathers." Since his ancestors were gentiles, Obadiah asked whether he could use that phrase. It also seems from the answer of Maimonides that the convert was not fully accepted as a Jew by some members of the Jewish community. Maimonides defends Obadiah and addresses him in a most respectful manner as follows: "Master and teacher, the intelligent and enlightened Obadiah, the righteous proselyte. . . . You are a great scholar and possess an understanding mind, for you have understood the issues and know the right way." Maimonides urges him to say in the prayers "Our God and God of our Fathers," because the proselyte "is a pupil of our father Abraham and all proselytes are members of his household. . . . Further, do not belittle your lineage, if we trace our descent to Abraham, Isaac, and Jacob, your connection is with Him by whose world the universe came into being." Maimonides also assures him, "A man who left his father and his mother and birthplace and the realm of his people at a time when they are powerful, who understood with his insight, and who attached himself to this nation which today is a despised people, the slaves of rulers, and recognized and knew that their religion is true and righteous . . . the Lord does not call you a fool, but intelligent and understanding, wise and walking correctly, a pupil of Abraham our Father" (*Encyclopedia Judaica*, 1977, pp. 1188–1189).

Not all were as generous in their attitude toward proselytes as was Maimonides. During the Middle Ages that brought on the Crusades, the pogroms, and the ghettos, Jewish distrust and fear of the outside world were intensified. Jews as a persecuted group developed a mystical definition of themselves as distinct from other peoples. Rabbi Judah Loew (1530–1609 CE), known as Maharal of Prague, was a leading spokesman. He postulated that "there is a metaphysical difference between Jew and gentile." According to Rabbi Loew, each people has an essence peculiar to itself. That essence and form expresses itself in a specific people's particular language, dress, food, and geography. A person cannot change his or her essence nor can he or she relinquish it voluntarily or even under duress. It is not a matter of choice for the person to make. What is true of an individual is also true of a group as a whole; an Israelite in relation to a gentile occupies a different dimension of existence.

Rabbi Loew's argument leads to a logical conclusion that no conversion could ever take place, but even Rabbi Loew left the door open to proselytes. He justified their acceptance into the Jewish community with the argument that a proselyte who, in spite of the hostile environment, seeks Judaism demonstrates a prior and an innate disposition toward Judaism. Therefore, that individual was never anything but Jewish. "Do not ask," he says, "how can a proselyte accept the Torah? Has he not an inadequate spiritual disposition? There is no difficulty at all. The fact is that he wishes to share the fate of Jews, and he converts, so he is absorbed into the people of Israel and acquires [all] its spiritual characteristics" (Sherwin, 1982, p. 103). In essence what Rabbi Loew conveys is that the Jewish people is a clearly defined and perfect entity, and thus additions could disturb that perfection. But even he acknowledged that a sincere proselyte does not disturb that perfection. Rabbi Loew maintains that the new Jew is not really a convert but in reality a Jew from his or her day of birth.

To the nonmystic, the position of Rabbi Loew may seem farfetched, but those who instruct proselytes or who come in contact with them do not dismiss that position lightly. Proselytes often volunteer an explanation for their conversion: "Ever since I remember I felt as if I were a Jew." Many search their family tree diligently hoping to discover a Jewish ancestor. Maimonides, the rationalist, and Loew, the mystic, seem to be on the opposite side of the spectrum. The former accepts the convert as long as all conversion requirements are met, while the latter apparently discourages proselytism. Yet both are in agreement that Judaism mandates the acceptance of true proselytes.

The personal identification of a sincere convert, as well as the dire dangers resulting from conversion to Judaism that lasted until modern times, can be encapsulated in the case of the Polish count Valentine Potocki, who lived in the last part of the eighteenth century. The Polish authorities were informed that the count had become a Jew. Potocki was burned at the stake, but not before he recited the prayer found in the daily morning service, "Blessed be You our Lord . . . who sanctifies your name before multitudes" (*Encyclopedia Judaica*, 1977, pp. 934–935). One of the legends about Count Potocki is that a priest came to his cell to plead with him to recant and save his soul from damnation. Potocki refused on the basis of his understanding of the revelation at Sinai. He explained to the priest that the Israelites made a solemn pledge at Sinai, "we shall hearken, and we shall do," and that there is also a tradition that prior to the Sinai event God offered the Torah to the other nations who refused the offer. Potocki reasoned that not all Jews accepted the Torah and similarly not all gentiles refused the offer. He considered himself to be one of the few gentiles whose soul made the pledge to God that he accepted the Torah; hence, "how can I recant such a pledge".

Why is there so much discussion about proselytism in the post-talmudic period despite the very few cases of conversion to Judaism? One could speculate that even in the darkest days of persecution against Jews, particularly during the Crusader period when hundreds of Jewish communities were destroyed, the eschatological hope that the world will embrace the God of Israel was not dimmed. Judaism as a universal faith was proclaimed by Jews three times a day.

That theological concept is contained in the prayer *Aleinu L'Shabbeach*—it is our duty to praise (the Lord of all things). The first paragraph emphasizes that Israel is God's chosen people; the second paragraph calls for a united humankind under the Kingship of the Almighty. The prayer, originally composed by a third-century Rabbi Rav, was recited only on the Jewish New Year, but in the twelfth century during the time of the Crusades it was included in all services where it continues to be recited three times daily. The two paragraphs in juxtaposition are a powerful theological statement. The Jew sees him- or herself as having a purer and more religious life than others ("He made our lot unlike that of other people," Harlow, 1985, p. 161) and, at the same time, proclaims that in a future sanctified world, the Jewish community will be open to all

("May everyone accept the rule of your Kingship," Harlow, 1985, p. 161).

Thus, it appears that when both the proselyte and the proselytizer were in danger of death, proselytism was discouraged. That fear is expressed by Solomon Luria, a contemporary of Rabbi Loew. "Now that we are in a country not our own . . . should one of Israel accept a convert, he is a rebel and is responsible for his own death. . . . Hence, I give warning that anyone who is a participant in such acceptance today, when the gentile kingdom is stringent in its attitude, let his blood be on his own head" (Katz, 1961, p. 145).

A strong statement, but, if one reads between the lines, if the Christian world would relent in the persecution of the proselyte and proselytizer, even Solomon Luria would open the doors of Judaism to the righteous proselyte.

In conclusion, it is evident that proselytism never ceased in Jewish life even during the centuries of the domination of the Christian church from Constantine in 315 CE until the French Revolution in 1789. Records of individual heroism both for the proselyte and the proselytizer are to be found during that period. The often stated current opinions that Judaism opposes proselytism may be the result of the understandable hesitation that for centuries the Jewish community has displayed toward the would-be converts because of the probability of tragic retaliation by the Christian authorities. The discouragement was not rooted in theology but in fear of political consequences.

MODERN PERIOD

Until the end of the eighteenth century, rabbinic discussions on conversions to Judaism were mostly theoretical in nature. Proselytism was proscribed by church law, and social contacts between Jews and gentiles were almost nonexistent. Jews lived behind ghetto walls and developed a self-contained community. Centuries of discrimination and ghettoization had led to a Jewish existence that was distinct from surrounding gentile cultures and had turned inward in its concerns. Customs, beliefs, and life-styles had been codified and enacted with fairly narrow standards. Although there were variations for some customs (Ashkenazi and Sephardi, for example), individuals generally followed the local form without reference to other variations. Jewish males, excluded from the education, thought, and life-styles that were part of the gentile world, focused their creative and intellectual energies on study of Jewish texts. Jewish females created stable home environments and supported family home rituals and holy days, especially the Sabbath.

This all changed in the modern period in Jewish history, which dates from the French Revolution in 1789. The revolution promised to usher in an age of "liberty, equality, and fraternity." Grudgingly, the new regime had to share these ideals with the Jews living in its midst. In the 1800s, as a result of the Napoleonic conquests, the social changes for the Jew brought about by the French Revolution spread beyond the borders of France. The ghetto walls in Western Europe crumbled, but with them the ethnic and religious cohesion of the Jewish community also began to erode. Suddenly, the external world was opened to Jews. Some clung ever more tightly to their Jewish world; some abandoned their Jewish identity entirely to join the mainstream of the gentile world; others sought to redefine Judaism and what it meant to be a Jew in order to have what they perceived to be the best of both worlds.

Actually, the modern period brought two interacting events into the Jewish community—emancipation, which gradually removed social barriers, and enlightenment, which introduced scientific and philosophical modes of thinking. In response to emancipation, some Jews moved out of the confines of the ghetto, going as far away as the Americas in order to enhance their economic and social status. These moves reduced their contact with community and religious leadership controls. In response to enlightenment, some Jewish leaders sought to redefine the beliefs and practices of Judaism to make them comparable with gentile life-styles and Christian religious practices. The resulting differences in interpretation eventually led to the formation of three major branches in Judaism— Reform, Conservative, and Orthodox. Reform Jews sought to make Judaism a fully modern religion. Conservative Jews sought to maintain traditional Judaism with some accommodation to modern life. Orthodox Jews resolved to retain the traditions and limit the effects of modernity. (For a more detailed analysis of the effects of emancipation and enlightenment, see the Fall 1989 issue of *Judaism,* which is devoted to this topic.)

As common Jews took advantage of their newly found freedom and engaged in educational, economic, and social contacts with their neighbors, and as many moved from Europe to the new frontiers of America, inevitably assimilation and mixed marriages became issues. The discussions in the Jewish community on proselytism, which had been dormant or, at the most, theoretical since 315 CE, were now on the Jewish communal agenda. Would an openness to proselytism encourage mixed marriages and with it a danger to Jewish survival, or would proselytism slow the attrition that was taking place in the Jewish community? Emancipation turned out to be a mixed blessing for the Jew. On one hand, Jews yearned for a life without pogroms and social ostracism, but, on the other hand, the ghetto had insulated Jews against the danger of assimilation. Emancipation now increased the likelihood of a minority being assimilated by the majority. Thus, the issue of assimilation/absorption once again was a concern. It was not a theoretical debate; answers were sought by Jews and gentiles alike.

In Europe, Napoleon Bonaparte, the emperor of France, convened a conference of Jewish notables in 1806 for the purpose of defining the role of the Jew in the modern world. That gathering was called the "Sanhedrin," evoking the image of the Jewish legislative and judicial body of the past. A series of issues were posed to the delegates, one of which dealt with mixed marriages. No easy answer was forthcoming. The delegates did not wish to appear parochial, since they sensed that protection attempts would not please Napoleon and could even jeopardize other fruits of emancipation, but they feared that to sanction intermarriage would send a wrong signal to Jewish young people indicating that out-marriages were permitted, which could cause a further exodus from the Jewish community. The compromise decided on was that whereas such marriages were not in conformity with Jewish laws, nevertheless civil marriages would be recognized as binding on Jews.

While another outcome of emancipation was the development of different branches in Judaism, during the early periods of emancipation there was unanimity of opinion that mixed marriages led to assimilation. The most radical Reform rabbis and the most stringent Orthodox rabbis deplored the growing tendency toward such marriages (see for example, Levenson, 1989). Conversion was not offered as an option. In 1880, Rabbi David Einhorn, a radical reformer, called for a total prohibition against such marriages, since "to lend a hand to the sanctification of mixed marriages is, according to my conviction, to furnish a nail to the coffin of a small race with a sublime mission" (cited by Davis, 1968, p. 181). In 1909 in the United States, the Central Conference of American Rabbis, the national organization of Reform rabbis, declared that a mixed marriage was "contrary to the tradition of the Jewish religion and should therefore be discouraged by the American Rabbinate" (Yearbook, p. 170).

If such was the attitude of Reform leadership, nothing less could be expected from the Orthodox. Thus, the late chief rabbi of the British Empire, Joseph H. Hertz, in his biblical commentary on Deuteronomy 7:3–4 "your daughter you shall not give to his son, nor his daughter shall you take for you son . . ." says, "In our own day, in conditions that are worlds asunder from those in Canaan of old, intermarriage is no less fatal to the continued existence of Israel." In support of his opinion, he quotes Rabbi Morris Joseph of England who in 1903 wrote, "Every Jew who contemplates marriage outside the pale must regard himself as paving the way to a destruction which would be final, as it would be the culminating disaster in the history of the Jewish people" (Hertz, 1938, p. 774).

These pronouncements, we know now, did not halt mixed marriages. The historian Arthur Hertzberg, an authority on the Emancipation period, points out "that every Jewish community since emancipation has had at least one member in three by the third generation marry a person whose religion at birth was non-Jewish" (1946, p. 48).

At the beginning of Jewish settlement in the United States, marriage between a Jew and a gentile was considered inevitable. Small Jewish communities have always found it difficult to maintain their identity and, over a period of years, tended to disappear into the mainstream. This was the case with U.S. Jews in the eighteenth and nineteenth centuries who were few in number and could not stem the tide of intermarriage or assimilation. People of marriageable age were afforded few choices for partners, and, in addition, there were available few community institutions that were essential to strengthen a sense of Jewish identity. The early American Jews assimilated easily into the majority culture and married outside of their faith. Hardly any contemporary American Jews can trace their ancestry to the early Jewish settlers of Spanish descent going back to the seventeenth or eighteenth centuries or to settlers of German descent going back to the nineteenth century. The prominent families of Spanish or German Jewry (for example, the Lazarus, Brandeis, Schiff, Warburg, Lehman, and Baruch families) with few exceptions are no longer part of the Jewish community. Assimilating in the American "melting pot" was the unwritten law of civic obligation. In the absence of a meaningful and organized larger

Jewish community, there was no one to wage a war with the problems of mixed marriages and assimilation or to take significant steps to stem the tide.

Some Jews defied the trend toward mixed marriages, but they did it at a great personal sacrifice, by deciding not to marry rather than to marry a gentile. One such person was Emma Lazarus, the poet whose famous lines, "Give me your tired, your poor . . ." grace the base of the Statute of Liberty. She lived in America in the middle of the nineteenth century when the Jewish community was small in number. She remained unmarried rather than sever her ties with the Jewish community. Her uncle, J. J. Lyons, was the spiritual leader of New York's Spanish and Portuguese Synagogue, which made it a rule that no rabbi was to officiate at any mixed marriage ceremony even when a conversion took place. It is noteworthy that Emma's sister, Ann, married a gentile and, since conversion was prohibited, severed all her connections with the Jewish people. Rebecca Graetz, whose father supported George Washington, remained unmarried even though she and Samuel Erwing, a minister's son, loved each other.

However, for the Jews who immigrated from Eastern Europe in the late nineteenth century and early twentieth century, the marriage of a Jew to a gentile was uncommon. The four million Jews who immigrated from Eastern Europe from 1881 to 1920 formed sizeable Jewish neighborhoods, spoke their own language, Yiddish, and socialized within their own community. Also because of their tragic experiences of pogroms and persecutions in Europe at the hands of Christians, they tended to maintain a distance from gentiles. Nor was contact with Jews encouraged by Christian churches. A parishioner had to get permission from his pastor to visit a house of worship not his own. In such a milieu, Jews married their own.

The children and grandchildren of East European Jewish immigrants, though educated in American schools and evidencing a high degree of Americanization, tended not to marry outside their faith. That tendency was reinforced during the Hitler period and its aftermath. The relatively few mixed marriages were treated as calamities by parents and as a betrayal of the Jewish faith and the Jewish people. The Holocaust, which destroyed one-third of world Jewry, and the establishment of Israel in 1948 highlighted the ethnic consciousness of the Jew that had the effect of temporarily stemming the oncoming tide of mixed marriages.

We know now, as Hertzberg feared, that in an open society

attrition from the Jewish community will take place. Why wasn't conversion to Judaism offered as an option in the early period of emancipation? We can only speculate. Could it be that Christian persecutions in the Middle Ages, lasting until the Emancipation, made the thought of a Jew marrying a gentile unacceptable to Jews? How can one be married to someone whose ancestors caused so much suffering to Jews? Another reason perhaps is that the rabbis were under the illusion that they exerted the same type of influence in an emancipated community as the rabbis of the ghetto whose pronouncements were law. However, such power could not be maintained in a open society where choice became a paramount option for individuals to exercise. One may wonder today what would have happened to the Sephardic Jewish community that settled in the United States in the 1600s whose descendents are almost all outside the Jewish community, or to the great number of the early German Jews who settled in the 1850s whose descendents likewise virtually disappeared, if conversion to Judaism had been available and encouraged at that time. Would the exodus from the Jewish community have been lessened?

As time passed and Jews had experience in living in an open society, some rabbis foresaw that viable outreach and conversion programs should be developed. Some began to believe that ways had to be found to make Judaism meaningful enough for gentiles to embrace, at least in cases of intermarriage. One such rabbi was Mordecai Kaplan, who in the 1930s, when the rate of intermarriage was less than 5 percent, wrote in his monumental study of the American Jewish community called *Judaism as a Civilization,*

> Jews must be prepared to reckon frankly and intelligently with intermarriage as a growing tendency which, if left uncontrolled, is bound to prove Judaism's undoing. They must realize that the power and vitality of a civilization are put to the test whenever the members of different civilizations come into social contact with each other. When the contacts result in intermarriage and children are born, the more vigorous civilization will be the one to which the children will belong (Kaplan, 1957, p. 413).

Not all heeded his call.

In 1935, just one year after *Judaism as a Civilization* was published, the *bet din* of Syrian Jews in America, an Orthodox homogeneous community alarmed at the increase of mixed marriages, believed that the only way to deal with intermarriage was to ban conversions. "We have observed the conditions prevailing in the general Jewish community where some youths left the haven of their faith and have assimilated with non-Jews: in certain cases they have made efforts to convert gentiles . . . an action which is absolutely invalid and worthless in the eyes of the law of our Torah." This statement was signed by the rabbis together with outstanding laymen of Syrian synagogues (cited by Lieberman, 1988, pp. 23–24).

Perhaps in a homogeneous community such bans can slow the attrition, but they certainly do not work generally among American Jews.

Egon Mayer, author of numerous articles, research reports, and books dealing with intermarriage and its affects on the Jewish community, estimates that "there are currently 350,000 Jews who are married to spouses who were not born Jews. These marriages produce between 400,000 and 600,000 children. Thus, about one million individuals (including the Jewish-born spouses) are directly involved in intermarriages between Jews and non-Jews" (1985, p. 10).

To the best of our knowledge, these statistics have not been challenged. The American Jewish community today is largely native born and the overwhelming majority of its youth are third, fourth, and even fifth generation American. Past barriers to complete integration with American life by and large have been dismantled. General acceptance of religious, ethnic, and racial diversities on the college campuses as well as the growing secularization of Jews and gentiles caused many to question the relevance of the ban against mixed marriages. Whereas previously intermarriage was viewed as a rebellion of isolated members of the Jewish community or as a means to enhance a Jew's social standing, today it is viewed as two people of different faiths falling in love. Also, it has become evident that, as far as the Jewish partner is concerned, an intermarriage does not necessarily represent a rejection of Judaism or the Jewish people. How are Jews facing the current realities of intermarriages?

Jewish attitudes toward intermarriage and toward conversion are not uniform. A multiplicity of views abound and range between the extremes of unqualified oppositon and enthusiastic welcome. The debate has become worldwide. It is recognized that the very existence of the Jewish people hinges on the outcome of the challenge that intermarriage poses for Jewry.

One side counsels extreme caution in probing the sincerity and especially the motivation of applicants for conversion. In this view, no less than incontrovertible evidence should be accepted; the potential convert must be moved by love for Judaism and the desire to fulfill all the commandments. This craving for Judaism must be so strong that there can be no question that the convert is "halachically like a newborn babe" (*Yebamot* 22a); that is, the convert must desire the way of Torah as a baby desires the mother's breast. This position would, for all practical purposes, do away with conversion, since studies show that more than 90 percent who initially seek to embrace Judaism do so, at least in part, for the sake of marriage.

Those who counsel strict requirements also set another condition that the proselyte needs to meet, the unconditional acceptance of Jewish ethnicity. The court must not only judge the veracity of the convert's statement that "Your God is my God," but also that "Your people are my people," as Ruth said to Naomi. Thus, during the initial interview with the *bet din,* the proselyte should be discouraged. The court that must point out the Jews' continuing oppressed status today could also add more questions to the traditional ones such as, "Can you as a gentile identify with the great tragedy of the Holocaust that befell the Jewish people? Can you appreciate the vital role that Israel plays in the life of a Jew? In more normal circumstances, can you feel comfortable with other Jews, engaging in Jewish humor, partaking of Jewish food, and celebrating with them?"

From this strict point of view, the argument that the loss of Jews from the Holocaust that annihilated one-third of world Jewry, the low Jewish fertility rate, or continuing assimilation could be replenished through proselytism is dismissed almost contemptuously. These authorities bolster opposition to conversion by quoting the unfriendly passages of the tradition, in spite of the fact that most of the passages are favorable toward the proselyte. The Holocaust should not serve, they say, as a pretext to replenish Jewish losses, but it should serve as an impetus to an even greater awareness of the uniqueness and separateness of the Jewish people. Proselytism should not be predicated on social concerns but on the historical and religious experiences of the Jewish people. The rate of intermarriage may increase unabated, but intermarried families should not be brought into the Jewish community, and conversion should not be offered as an option except for a very small number who can demonstrate an unqualified acceptance of Judaism. Great obstacles are placed in the path of prospective converts.

In order to convert to Judaism, a gentile must find a sponsoring rabbi who will supervise a course of study and eventually perform the conversion ceremony and certification. Among rabbis today, conversion has become the focal point of conflict among the traditions. The "Who is a Jew?" question for traditionally oriented rabbis is answered, "Only those persons with a fully *halachic* [that is, Orthodox] conversion." In Israel, the Orthodox rabbinate regularly attempts to exclude non-Orthodox converts under the Law of Return, defining converts from Reform and Conservative rabbis as gentiles. Recently when exclusion measure failed, the Israeli rabbis sought to stamp converts' identification cards with a mark identifying them as converts (that is, not "real" Jews). The Israeli Supreme Court has rejected this identification attempt, so the Israeli legislature continues to be the focus of exclusion attempts by the Orthodox rabbinate in Israel.

In both 1935 and 1984, the Orthodox leadership made a formal statement opposing conversion for marriage (Mayer 1985, p. 216). Converts for any reason are not welcomed by Orthodox rabbis, but, in fact, are discouraged. Most potential converts are not aware that rabbis traditionally must reject them at least three times to test their sincerity. If the potential convert is from a Christian religious background where converts are both warmly welcomed and even sought, this rejecting atmosphere is quite a surprise. Some rabbis do accept the Talmud's more positive view of *gerim* (righteous gentiles, converts) as being dearer to God than Israel because the proselyte "accepts Judaism without witnessing even one miracle whereas Israel experienced God's voice." Most, however, convey an ambivalence about the value of converts; many will not aid a potential convert at all. Recent attempts to systemically handle converts initiated by some Reform and Conservative rabbinical groups are the exception rather than the rule.

One modern convert who managed to overcome all the obstacles placed in his path was Father Kenneth Charles Cox, known by his Hebrew name as Abraham Isaac Carmel. In an article written just prior to his death, citing his unpublished book, *My Chosen People,* he recalls the difficulties he encountered. "A proselyte, if he tries to live up to his calling will re-live within his brief span the discrimination, hostility, and callous cynicism experienced down the ages by those whom he has chosen as his people. Most cruel of all, he will find much of his suffering within that very family from which he had hoped to draw strength and consolation" (1988).

Are the obstacles necessary? Paradoxically, although Jewish law is cited as the excuse for discriminating against proselytes and sociological arguments are said to be unacceptable, in fact it is social reality that determines the interpretation and not Jewish law. In Jewish law it is not at all clear that conversion for the sake of marriage is an unacceptable reason. The commentary *Sifrei Kohen,* known popularly as the "shach," on the passage from the authoritative law code *Yoreh Deah* 208 paragraph 12, states that "when a proselyte comes before the Jewish court, and we know that he or she wishes to join the Jewish people for the sake of marriage, the court should probe farther, and, if the person is sincere, conversion can take place." Thus, legitimacy is to be determined by the judgment of the court based on the perception of the judges as to whether or not the potential convert has a sincere basis for conversion beyond the desire for marriage.

To further our point about current controversies on conversions, we cite opinions by three prominent Orthodox rabbis whose credentials are accepted by the vast majority in the Orthodox community, which demonstrate that there are wide disagreements even within orthodoxy about how to apply the laws to the would-be convert.

Rabbi Immanuel Jakobovits, the present chief rabbi of the United Kingdom, states unequivocally, "The conditions for admission to Judaism are simple enough in definition. It is open to any person irrespective of race, color, or previous creed." If he had stopped at that point, it would have signaled an openness toward proselytism. His additional statement shut the door in the face of candidates for conversion: "The criterion is the love for Judaism and not for the Jewish [partner]" (1989, p. 210). It is noteworthy that under his spiritual leadership conversions in England under Orthodox auspices are almost nonexistent. Rabbi Jakobovits calls conversion "the most delicate heart operation to which a person could ever submit . . . and the [convert] must be adequately prepared to undergo such an operation" (*Jewish Chronicle,* 1988, p. 23). These attitudes are reflected in the fact that in England there are no organized courses for conversion under Orthodox auspices. In five years, the *bet din* dealt with 610 applicants, but only 101 conversions were approved.

Another scholar with indisputable Orthodox credentials takes the opposite point of view. Rabbi Joseph B. Soloveichik, known recently as "Ha Rav," "The Rabbi," by students and by the Orthodox community, in an interview approved the Reform policy of active encouragement of conversion to Judaism. Soloveichik states:

> We don't have the strength to convince a young man or woman who has fallen in love with a non-Jew. There is no formula—not even the best Jewish education—which is able to function as a shield in the face of this phenomenon. After the fact, the possibility of dissuasion is very weak. . . . The correct way is specifically the way of the Reform (and I am sure many of my Orthodox friends will stone me on account of what I am saying)—of course with Orthodox content. . . . We must develop programs and methods to integrate them under the wings of God's presence and to make them good Jews. . . . There are Jews whose wives, born gentiles, have brought their [Jewish] husbands back to Judaism . . . (1986, p. 7).

The distinguished halachist, authority on Jewish law, Rabbi Ben-Zion Meir Hai Uziel, a former chief rabbi of the Sephardic community in Israel, replying to a question of proselytism for the sake of marriage sent to him by the then chief rabbi of Istambul, quoted the authoritative code of Jewish law (*Yoreh Deah* 268:12), "that the motives of converts must be examined lest they convert for the sake of marriage" (cited by Angel, 1972, p. 108). But Rabbi Uziel adds significantly the following: "Since in our generation intermarriage is widespread in civil courts, we should permit them to be performed Jewishly, for otherwise the Jewish partner lives in sin, and the children may eventually be lost to Judaism (cited by Angel, 1972, pp. 269–270).

It becomes apparent that currently the divergent opinions on conversion for the sake of marriage involve not so much Jewish law but the emotional attitude of scholars and their perception as to what is best for their communities. Rabbi Jakobovits' concern is with English Jewry being assimilated and weakened by the majority culture, while Rabbi Uziel, responding to a rabbi from Istambul, knows that a Jewish community is in no danger of being assimilated in a Moselm society, and, thus, the objective becomes to stop whatever attrition there may be in the Jewish community. It is also possible that Rabbi Soloveichik, who for many years occupied a pulpit in Boston while teaching in academia, was not at all frightened by the prospect of absorption of converts into the American Jewish community.

The rabbis are more united in a negative stance toward non-conversionary marriages. Orthodox rabbis are instructed not to perform *any* religious ceremonies for mixed marrieds, the *mesadrim* (deacons) are to give no honor or recognition to the Jewish partner of an intermarriage, and a mixed-married Jew is not to be buried in a Jewish ceremony (Mayer, 1985, p. 216). Since a Jewish marriage is viewed as a covenant between two persons "under the laws of Moses and of Israel," a mixed marriage cannot be religiously valid. Officiation at the marriage ceremony is viewed as approval of mixed intermarriage, and only some Reform rabbis are willing to be present. Mixed marrieds usually have a "Jewish-style" ceremony with a Christian officiating, or they have a civil ceremony (Diamant, 1985, pp. 36–40).

There is serious controversy among the rabbis also as to the proper response to mixed-married couples and to their offspring. Some favor rejection like the Orthodox stance just mentioned. Others, particularly in the Reform camp, believe an outreach is appropriate to try to engender as much Jewish practice and identity as possible. In 1983, the Reform's Central Conference of American Rabbis went so far as to support recognition of the offspring of mixed marriages as being Jewish whether or not the mother converted. Traditional Judaism recognizes only the offspring of a Jewish mother as being Jewish. The Reform rabbis qualified this ruling by saying that the child of a Jewish father in a mixed marriage would be accepted as Jewish if the child was circumcised, had a Hebrew name, engaged in Torah study, had a *bar* or *bat mitzvah*, and was confirmed, acts showing a personal commitment to Judaism (Silberman, 1985, pp. 321–322). Conservative rabbis have just recently begun to endorse outreach to intermarrieds with the goal of converting the gentile spouse (Kalb and Weinshanker, 1987; Silverstein, 1987).

While not all rabbis severely oppose intermarriage, especially where there is a conversion of the gentile to Judaism, a strongly negative view remains.

In the modern context, religious practice and ethnic identity have become separate concerns even for the rabbis. It is often believed that the attraction that gentiles feel for Judaism is the alleged warmth of the Jewish family and the network that Jews provide for each other throughout the world. Jews are concerned for Soviet

Jews, the State of Israel, the poor in their midst, and the well-being of fellow Jews. This type of ethnic identity and concern seems to be largely lacking in the gentile community. Ethnicity also means being part of a civilization. As Nathan Taxer points out, ethnic identification is a "people who feel they have a common identity and common cultural heritage, who may feel they are of a common descent, who may speak a common language, who may inhabit a contiguous stretch of territory, and who may on occasion form a nation-state" (cited by Edelheit, 1957, p. 82). Gentiles may find Jewish history and family and community solidarity a greater attraction than traditional religious practice. At the same time, religious practice may be easier for an outsider to take on than an ethnic identification.

Jews ask, "Could a convert *feel* Jewish?" According to some, a convert can never be absorbed into the Jewish community. There is an axiom among Jews, "A goy remains a goy." At the first argument, the gentile spouse in anger will surely say, "You're a dirty Jew."

One cannot deny that ethnicity remains a vital difference between the Jewish and gentile community even in America. Figure 2.1 lists major areas of difference between these communities in the United States today. Major differences are found in family formation, structure, and interaction; residential and socioeconomic patterns; values and life-styles; and community concerns. While differences in religious involvement between Christians and Jews have lessened, Jewish ethnicity retains its distinct character. Even the religious cycles create ethnic-related differences in rituals, foods, and the calendar of family gatherings.

We thus see that in a free society, devoid of political or legal obstacles to full integration, the rate of intermarriage has been increasing and is likely to continue to do so. *Halacha* (Jewish law), although involved, plays a relatively minor role in the debate of various Jewish religious spokesmen and scholars. Today, the overriding concern is whether or not an openness to converts will strengthen or weaken the Jewish community. The disagreements about intermarriage and conversion are not necessarily along "denominational" lines; there is significant disagreement within each camp. While Reform Judaism in the past stated its total opposition to intermarriage, today Reform rabbis are highly involved in outreach programs to mixed couples, trying to integrate them into the community. While a minority of Reform rabbis perform mixed marriages without conversion, the majority do so only after the

FIGURE 2.1
SUMMARY OF JEWISH ETHNIC AND RELIGIOUS
DIFFERENCES FROM THE U.S. CHRISTIAN MAJORITY

Community Cohesion—The extent and depth of shared solidarity, interaction, aspirations, status, lifestyles, and cultural values.

Migration—Jews are concentrated in urban areas and in certain regions and states; 60% move in a 10-year period; they tend to move to high-density Jewish areas; there is lower synagogue attendance for young movers for at least 3 years after they move.

Residential Concentration and Interaction—65% of Jews live in areas of medium concentration of Jews, 15% in high concentration areas; 85% say most of their friends are Jews.

Living Arrangements—Jews are more likely to live alone if not married except older Jewish females who are more likely to live with relatives; unmarried non-Jews are more likely to live with relatives (35% unmarried gentile males living with relatives vs. 7% Jewish males, 33% unmarried gentile females living with relatives vs. 13% Jewish females); Jewish males 30–60 years of age are more likely to live within a marital family (96% Jews vs. 88% non-Jews).

Socioeconomic Patterns—Jews have higher levels of education with less variability in education as a group, and have higher incomes; Jews are concentrated in professional and managerial positions; a higher percentage of Jews are self-employed; 10% of Jews are workers vs. 50% non-Jews; Jewish females' occupational concentration is similar to Jewish males' pattern, and they have experienced a quicker rise in status than non-Jewish females; there is higher upward mobility between generations for Jews (⅔ of Jewish workers' children are professionals or managers, ⅔ of non-Jewish workers' children are also workers).

Marriage Endogamy—Jews still have considerably higher in-marriage rates than other ethnic-religious groups; there is an increase in intermarriage, but 30% convert to Judaism; 60% of Jews are strongly concerned about the Jewishness of their grandchildren; intermarrieds' Jewish expression converges with the Jewish community especially with that of younger Jews.

Marriage and Family Formation—Jews have a higher marriage rate (for 30–44-year-old males 81% of Jews vs. 74% of non-Jews are married, for females 87% of Jews vs. 65% of non-Jews are married); Jews marry later (males 25 years for Jews vs. 23 for non-Jews, females 22 for Jews vs. 21 for gentiles); the age range for first marriage is less variable for Jews (⅔ of males marry between 22 and 29, females between 20 and 25); higher-income Jewish males marry later (27 years old vs. 24 for lower-income Jewish males); Jews have a lower divorce and separation rate (3% vs 15% for non-Jews; in the 45–59 age range 96% of Jews are in their first marriage vs. 84% of non-Jews)

Childbearing—For a century the fertility rate for Jews has been lower than for non-Jews; Jews plan and attain their desired family size with extreme accuracy; 15% have 1 child, 50% have 2 children, 30% have 3 children; 4% of Jews want 4 or more children, 20% of white ethnics want 4 or more; Jews have later childbearing because of educational involvements; better educated Jewish females have more children than educated non-Jewish females (2.5 children for Jews vs. 2.2 for gentiles) and more than lesser educated Jewish females; Jewish mothers are more likely to work but also have larger families than non-Jewish working mothers.

Religious Observances—¾ of Jews identify with one of the branches of Judaism; ¾ attend a synagogue service sometime each year; 80% observe some personal home rituals; ⅓ belong to a synagogue; 70% of Reform children identify as Reform, 46% of Conservative children identify as Conservative, the rest as Reform; there is a growing similarity of shared religious identity between the generations.

Jewish Values—More than non-Jews, Jews value interaction with other Jews, equality of all people, pleasure in this life, family security, inner harmony, independence in thought and action, being intellectual and logical, health concerns; Jews place less emphasis on being obedient, being polite, achieving personal salvation, and forgiving others.

Ethnic/Religious Styles—Jews differ in the following: Communication Patterns (confrontational, argumentative, rational, loud, expressive, passionate), Emphasis on Independence, Emphasis on Education, Authority Sources (rabbinical, science), Holiday Celebrations (Rosh Hashanah, Yom Kippur, Hanukah, Pesach), Wedding Arrangements (contractual nature, *Ketubah,* various customs; for example, the *Hupah* and glass-breaking), Child-oriented Ceremonies (*Brit,* Hebrew name, *Bar/Bat Mitzvah* as behavior not belief affirmation), Grief Handling (*Shiva,* no wake, *Kaddish,* Yahrzeit), Language (Hebrew, Yiddish, Ladino), The Calendar (year, months lunar), Traditional Dress and Practices by Orthodox, Sacred Texts (Hebrew Bible, Siddur, Talmud), Diet (Kosher, no pork, fasts, unleavened bread for Pesach), Home Rituals (candle lighting, prayers, songs, foods, wine, *hallah*), the Sabbath, Songs and Dance, Religious Objects (*shofar,* ark, menorah, candles, *mezuzah, tallit, kipah, tefillin,* Torah scrolls, etc.), *Aliyah, Mikvah.*

Issues of Concern—More than other groups, Jews are concerned about world events, Israel, the Holocaust, anti-Semitism, refuseniks, civil rights, the December Dilemma, charity, moral-ethical issues, who is a Jew, intermarrieds and convert integration, assimilation, attempts to convert Jews, and Jews for Jesus/Messianic Jews; Jews because of their educational and occupational positions are on the forefront of social change.

gentile partner converts to Judaism. All conservative rabbis require conversion including circumcision and immersion as a prerequisite for marriage. Orthodoxy, while in theory accepting conversion, in practice tends to discourage conversion to Judaism. However, as we previously indicated even with Orthodoxy, there is a recognition that the tide of intermarriage cannot be stanched and that conversion is to be offered as an option. The convert to Orthodoxy is held to the strictest standards of practice, must be immersed in a *mikvah,* and, if male, circumcised or nicked for a drop of blood to seal the Abrahamic identity.

CONCLUSION

We have looked at the different periods in Jewish history, alternately marked by collective feelings of security and insecurity. Our hypothesis has been that the status of the Jewish people at a given time was reflected in their attitudes toward proselytism. When establishing a new religion, the partiarchs prohibited intermarriage. As the early Hebrews began to view themselves as masters of their own destinies, particularly in a sovereign Jewish state as in the period of the First Commonwealth, there was little concern that proselytes would change the nature of the Jewish community and thus there was oppenness toward the *ger.* During much of that period, we have no evidence of any conversion ceremony.

During periods of foreign domination or oppression in exile, there was rising concern that newcomers to the community would introduce foreign elements in the Jewish faith and would lead the Jewish partner astray, and thus strict rules were applied. In its ghettoization, the community remained theoretically open to converts but practically closed because of the strictness imposed by Christianity.

In an open society, such as ours, both religious and ethnic issues emerge and a variety of interpretations have developed. The concern of the Orthodox rabbinate is to maintain the strict observance of *halacha* in the face of a society that encourages assimilation. Will the convert maintain a Jewish home, a Sabbath observance, dietary laws, family purity, and the rest of the 613 commandments? Absorption, it is believed, will occur only in a tightly controlled community. Accordingly, conversion is rare in the Orthodox faith community. On the other hand, both the Conservative and Reform movements are hopeful that the process of conversion will help tie both the gentile convert and Jewish spouse to the community. In their view, the ultimate success of that absorption process will be determined by both religious commitments and by ethnic identification and involvement. Will converts identify with Jewish issues, live in neighborhoods with a substantial Jewish population, have mostly Jewish friends, support Jewish causes, educate their children in religious schools, and become members in synagogues and Jewish organizations, thus adding to the community once they are encouraged to join the religion? Both Conservative and Reform communities believe so and thus have sought to open Judaism to gentiles.

SUMMARY OF RABBINIC CONCERNS

Our discussion in this chapter has raised a variety of concerns about converts and intermarriage. These issues are the major ones that need to be answered by studies including ours. Figure 2.2 summarizes these concerns under the categories of religious, religious-ethnic, and peoplehood-ethnic concerns. In the religious domain, rabbis question both the role of Jews in seeking converts and the religious procedures and practices to be required of converts. In the religious-ethnic area, rabbis are concerned about the effects of intermarriage on the Jewish community. And in the peoplehood-ethnic focus, rabbis address the additional issues of cultural identification, sensing that modern Christian converts may be approaching Judaism as a religion only.

Our conclusion is that throughout history the answer for the rabbis as to whether "your people can become my people" depends upon the prevailing view of the conditions for the Jewish community itself. When assimilation and thereby loss of Jews is feared, the community tightens its controls, and when the community is viewed as strong enough to absorb outsiders, controls are loosened. In the current U.S. context, assimilation is generally viewed as a threat by Jewish leaders. However, some believe conversion of the gentile partner in situations of intermarriage to be a viable answer to reducing losses. Rabbis of this optimistic view are engaged in designing conversion programs that will provide the impetus for the gentile to be absorbed into the Jewish (religious and ethnic) community. Are these programs successful?

We turn now to our data to try to throw light on these complex questions.

FIGURE 2.2
SUMMARY OF CURRENT ISSUES ABOUT CONVERTS
RAISED BY THE RABBIS

Religious

Should Judaism engage in "missionary" activities?

What reasons/proof are needed to accept a convert?

How much of the traditions must gentiles know and accept before conversion?

What ritual acts are required for legitimization of conversion?

What level of religious practice and involvement should be expected of converts?

Do converts have full access to Israel's covenantal relationship?

What effects do intermarriage (mixed and conversionary) have on the sanctification of the home?

Will converts import Christian/pagan practices into Judaism?

Religious-Ethnic

Will a lenient policy toward conversion increase the intermarriage rate?

What responsibility toward the convert and Jewish spouse does the Jewish community have?

Can the Jewish community absorb massive outside influences?

Will converts offset assimilation losses?

Does intermarriage, even a conversionary one, indicate a weak commitment to Judaism?

What is the importance of the initial motive for conversion (especially marriage)?

Aren't there enough problems in marriage without dissimilar religious backgrounds adding to the possibility of divorce?

Peoplehood-Ethnic

Can converts identify with the entire historical experience of Jews (Holocaust, diaspora, anti-Semitism, etc.)?

How well can/do converts integrate into Jewish community and friendship networks?

Will converts support Jewish causes?

What effect will converts' ties to Christian and gentile relatives and friends have?

Can conversionary intermarrieds pass a Jewish identity and commitment on to their children?

3

Study Findings for Participants in the Chicago Area Introduction to Judaism Course

INTRODUCTION

Our previous discussion has addressed the context of concerns to which our study responds. Thus far research on converts is largely confined to the work of Egon Mayer. His work draws on information from converts of varying community backgrounds and conversion instruction. The conversion process is not a systematic or standardized one throughout the United States. Prospective converts must find a rabbi with whom to study, but the content and length of study vary. Our data are based on a group of persons who participated in a common program in one community. Thus, we have a unique opportunity to learn the outcomes from an organized effort on the part of the Jewish community to attract and prepare converts.

HISTORY OF THE INTRODUCTION TO JUDAISM COURSE

Until recently intermarriage was considered an act of rejection [of the religion and of the group]. Among traditionalists, not only was intermarriage not condoned, but the Jewish spouse was considered "dead" and his of her family observed many of the traditional rites of mourning. . . . Intermarriage, even when involving conversion, was perceived as harmful to the Jewish people which has a strong sense of corporate identity (Waxman, 1983, p. 174).

In 1973, the first jointly sponsored formal course for would-be converts to Judaism was organized in Chicago by the Conservative and Reform rabbinates. Until that year, Chicago, the fourth largest Jewish community in the United States, numbering in its metropolitan area about 253,000 Jews, had no such program. Prior to 1973, since neither the lay people nor the rabbis were concerned about intermarriage (which they believed affected an insignificant percentage of Jewish marriages), there had been feeble attempts to deal with conversion to Judaism. By 1973, it was evident that mixed marriages were occurring in ever-increasing numbers and that a communitywide effort to reach gentile partners was essential. Previous attempts to prevent mixed marriages had focused on dissuading the Jewish partner, but the community began to believe that social forces were making it futile to continue to try to prevent such marriages from taking place. As one Jewish parent put it: "I would make every effort to show him the error of his way. Then I'd accept the situation, but I'd be broken-hearted" (Schwartz, 1970, p. 117).

Gradually, the leadership began to believe that in order to preserve a Jewish identity in the home and to retain the next generation, the community's energies should be expended in offering to the gentile partner the option of conversion. Not all the rabbis agreed with a proselytizing approach, though even in Orthodox circles, disowning is out. For example, Rabbi Winkler advises:

Threatening to disown a child may succeed only in rare cases and in instances when the interdating child is so emotionally attached to the parents that such threats would bear the desired results. But parents take great risks in attempting any action and should consult an experienced rabbi or counsellor first. Today, more often than not, children are not into "guilt" but we're all okay, just live and let live. But by maintaining a positive relationship with a child, the chances of reaching them, or at least rescuing future generations of Jews, are much higher (1986, p. 6).

He does not, however, advise parents to attend the wedding, even a civil ceremony, lest that be viewed as acceptance.

The issue of conversion was debated at rabbinical meetings. Some felt that by facilitating and encouraging conversion, rabbis in fact would be signaling to Jews that it was acceptable to seek partners outside their faith; others argued that a conversion program would counteract the attrition taking place in the community because of intermarriage and that serious converts would strengthen rather than weaken Jewish life.

In 1973, the rabbis in Chicago worked out a compromise. The Conservative and Reform rabbinates agreed to launch a common class for potential converts; however, no publicity was to be given to the course. Only those individuals sponsored by a rabbi would be admitted to the course, which would be called "An Introduction to Judaism." The actual ceremony of conversion would be in the hands of the sponsoring rabbi, who would be free to require additional study, practice, and involvement time of the candidate.

The first class met in the fall of 1973 for ten weeks of instruction with each session meeting ninety minutes. Soon additional classes were added so that by the time of this study, ten classes were held each year. The length of the class was expanded to fifteen weeks with two hours per session. Each class enrolled twenty to thirty candidates. The Jewish partner was encouraged to attend the sessions also, and most partners do participate. More than two thousand candidates have enrolled in the course since 1973.

While fifteen weeks may not be adequate to expose a person to the vast treasury of Jewish knowledge and experience, the course introduces the candidate to basic Jewish thought, practices, and community life issues. The candidate is provided fundamental information on which to base further study. Major areas covered include definitions of Jewishness, Jewish theology, worship forms, holiday and Sabbath observances, family and life cycle rituals, highlights of Jewish history including the Holocaust and the establishment of the State of Israel, the relationship of Judaism and other religions (particularly Christianity), the various movements in Judaism, and current Jewish community issues. In addition, recently a portion of each session has been devoted to imparting a reading knowledge of Hebrew for the purpose of the individual's being able to follow a synagogue worship service and to recite basic prayers (the *Shema* and the candle, wine, and bread blessings).

In addition to the class, the sponsoring rabbi meets with the candidate at regular intervals, during which time the candidate's concerns and readiness and the conversion requirements are explored. During the time of study, the candidate is expected to participate regularly in synagogue services and activities as well as to be involved in the Jewish community. Figure 3.1 summarizes the main components of the course; the full cirriculum was developed by Rabbi Joseph Amos Edelheit. This conversion program remains

FIGURE 3.1
COMPONENTS OF THE INTRODUCTION TO JUDAISM COURSE SPONSORED BY THE CHICAGO ASSOCIATION OF REFORM RABBIS AND THE CHICAGO REGION OF THE RABBINICAL ASSEMBLY*

1. Who is a Jew
   —Definitions—social, biological, *halachic;* uniqueness; culture and language; secular, Israeli, religious Jews

2. God, the Bible, the Covenant
   —Jewish ideas of God; belief vs. practice; creed; role of *Shema*
   —Torah vs. Old Testament; Torah and covenant; *Tanach*
   —Significance of covenant, being chosen, covenant and *mitzvot*

3. Rabbinic Judaism: Talmud, Midrash, Basic Theology
   —Oral vs. written Law, Talmud and its role
   —Midrash role for *Tanach,* importance of homilies and theology
   —Rabbinic Judaism, *Shulchan Aruch,* Responsa, rabbinic theology

4. Prayer
   —Jewish prayer, liturgy, role of Hebrew in prayer, *tallit* and *tefillin*
   —*Yetzer hatov* and *yetzer harah, teshuva* and *het, Keva* and *Kavanah*

5. Living as a Jew I: Home, Synagogue, Community
   —Essentials of a Jewish home, *mezzuzah, kashrut,* kosher
   —Origins and function of synagogue, Sabbath and festival celebrations, role of family and home
   —Role of Jewish Federation, *K'lal Israel* and *tzedakah,* Jewish education

6. Living as a Jew II: Life Cycle *Mitzvot,* Family
   —Characteristics of the Jewish family, stereotypes, intermarriage family relationships
   —*Brit Milah,* naming, *bar/bat mitzvah,* Jewish wedding, Jewish mourning

7. The Shabbat, the High Holidays
   —Meaning/role of Shabbat, Shabbat rituals and observances
   —*Slichot,* Rosh Hashanah, Yom Kippur observances

8. The Pilgrimage Festivals, the Minor Festivals, the Fasts
   —Pesach, Shavuot, and Sukkot observances; Simchat Torah
   —Purim, Hanukah, Tishah B'av, T'u Bishevat

9. Judaism and Christianity
   —Jewish view of Jesus, Messiah and Messianic Era; relationship to Christianity; view of "missionizing;" fate of the dead

10. Anti-Semitism and the Holocaust
    —Classic myths/stereotypes about Jews; deicide, blood libel, desecration
    of the host, usury, Protocols of the Elders of Zion, worldwide conspiracy
    of Jews charges; anti-Semitism today, role of Anti-Defamation League,
    American Jewish Congress, American Jewish Committee
    —*Shoah,* historical background, ramifications of 12 million humans/6
    million Jews killed, Yom Ha-Shoah

11. Zionism and the State of Israel
    —Development and role of Zionism, why the land of Israel, diaspora
    —The U.N. partition; War of Independence, Eichmann Trial, the Six-Day
    War, and Intifada; Yom Ha-Atzmaut

12. How Jews Observe Judaism: The Four Movements within Judaism
    —Shtetl vs. Emancipation, the major movements—Reform, Conservative,
    Orthodox, Reconstructionist, *halacha.*

---

*A copy of the Introduction to Judaism syllabus is available from Dr. Forster upon
request.

rather unique, although a few other communities, notably Los
Angeles, Boston, and Denver, have attempted to develop a systematic approach. No study has been done specifically on converts from
the other programs.

The Chicago experience provides us a "natural experiment" in
order to gain more information on the situation of converts. The
group was exposed to a roughly similar preparation and joined the
same metropolitan population in a major Jewish center. Because
many settled in the same area, a study covering fifteen years of
experiences was feasible. Hence, our study was designed to utilize
this unique opportunity. The next section briefly explains important, though a bit technical, information on how the study was put
into operation.

STUDY DESIGN

In order to gain as complete a picture as possible, given our resources, we decided to utilize a questionnaire that would be mailed
to former students of the course and given to current participating
students. We also felt it was important to gain information from the
partners of the present and former students. Since the questionnaire
had not as a whole been used in any previous study and since only
bare-bones information was available on practices by Jews (nothing
on beliefs of Jews), we queried a small sample of religiously oriented

born Jews as a base against which to compare our students and their partners. Finally, we got information from some current students at the beginning and at the end of the course in order to see the effects, if any, of the introductory experience.

Since our information was gathered by questionnaires, a word on their construction is in order. Where possible, questions used and found important in other studies were incorporated. Where measures did not exist, we constructed questions. We decided to sacrifice brevity for depth so that our questionnaires were a bit detailed and took forty to sixty minutes to complete. While the length undoubtedly reduced our return rate somewhat, we felt it was more important to gain detailed information from those who did respond. We used two basic versions of the questionnaires. The version we mailed to former students provided the core questions we asked the currently enrolled students; the version we used with the partners provided the core for the questions we asked of the born Jews. In all, we had seven questionnaire versions:

Former Student/Convert (mailed to persons who had completed the course between 1973 and 1987)

Pre-Course Student (given the first class session of the Introduction Course)

Post-Course Student (given the last day of class to the same classes that answered the pre-questionnaire)

Post-Course-Only Student (given the last day of class to classes that had not been given a pre-questionnaire)

Partner (mailed to partners of former students who had responded to the questionnaire and indicated their partners' willingness to respond)

Partner Course (given to partners of students in the above class situations)

Born Jew (mailed to area synagogue members of selected Conservative and Reform synagogues who were identified by their rabbis as born Jews)

Names and addresses on file for the Introduction to Judaism course were used to generate mailings. Volunteers transferred the name and address information to cards, checked names in city and suburban phone directories, called sponsoring rabbis for information, prepared a final list for mailing, prepared address labels, stuffed and labeled envelopes, handled the mailings and follow-ups, and cared for the incoming returns. Of our original list of 2,692 names, we mailed 963 questionnaires, of which 126 were returned as unforwardable, and gained 407 returns for a 49 percent rate, an acceptable return. We used two follow-up mailings—the first a reminder letter, the second a new questionnaire—to increase our return.

Former students returning questionnaires were asked if they had a partner who would be willing to help in the study. Questionnaires were sent to the 199 partners so identified, with 129 returns (a 65 percent return rate).

Those candidates attending the Introduction to Judaism course during the Fall and Spring 1987–1988, a total of seven classes, were requested to participate in the study described to them by Dr. Forster at the first or last class. The rabbis who assisted with this study provided the last forty minutes of class for students to answer the questionnaires. At the same time, partners attending the class were asked to fill out a questionnaire. Most class participants did fill out a questionnaire for the study. The participation rate was about 95 percent.

Rabbis at five "typical" Conservative and Reform synagogues in the city and suburbs were enlisted to submit names and addresses of their born Jew congregants. In order to balance the sample somewhat, we requested that they give us about an equal number of persons in the 20 to 35, 35 to 55, and over 55 age groups, and, if possible, marital pairs. We mailed questionnaires to those Jews so named, asking the pair to each fill out a questionnaire. Our return rate was about 75 percent for Conservative Jews and 45 percent for Reform Jews.

From these various data sources our findings are based on the numbers of participants shown in Table 3.1. We will look in more detail at the four student groups in the next section of this chapter. We will examine the details of the other groups and look at comparisons in the next chapter. Here we will focus on the data describing former students who have converted to Judaism.

All of the groups were asked for the same basic core of information on background, beliefs, practices, and child socializing. The areas we measured are:

Background characteristics
   PUSH—liberalizing influences helping to make Judaism a possible and attractive option for gentiles and, for Jews, relationships to Christians
   PULL—attachments to the Jewish community

TABLE 3.1
CATEGORIES OF STUDY PARTICIPANTS

Major Categories	Subcategory Number	Subtotal Number	Total Number*
Former Students			407
Converted Total		323	
Females	258		
Males	65		
Converted Reform		298	
Females	155		
Males	43		
Conververted Conservative		111	
Females	98		
Males	21		
Not Converted		84	
Females	32		
Males	52		
Pre-Course Students			88
Females	60		
Males	28		
Post-Course Students			38
Post-Course-Only			
Students			43
Females	34		
Males	9		
Partner Course			110
Reform	60		
Conservative	38		
Partners of Converts			136
Reform		82	
Conservative		46	
Born Jews			149
Reform		40	
Females	22		
Males	18		
Conservative		99	
Females	53		
Males	46		

*Subtotals may not add up to the totals because of missing responses and "other" choices.

Intervening
    Study activities (for students only)
    Current Jewish relationships
Outcomes
    Jewish beliefs held—theological, personal, ethnic
    Knowledge of Jewish community resources
    Importance of Jewish involvements
    Jewish practices—religious, sociocultural
    Socialization of own children—religious, sociocultural
    Context and consequences of intermarriage and of conversion, if any (for students only)
    Personal reflections about Jews and Judaism (several openended questions at the end of each questionnaire)[1]

The reader should be aware of the following factors. Since the mailed questionnaire was lengthy, our respondents are likely to be the more interested and committed former students. We do not know the characteristics of those who did not respond; however, assuming student characteristics have been relatively stable over time, we can get a sense of who they are from our data drawn from the ongoing classes, though we cannot be sure of nonrespondents' current involvements and practices.

What we do know is the characteristics of a substantial group of born gentiles who were concerned enough about their role vis-à-vis the Jewish community and Judaism to participate in a study course about Judaism, 79 percent of whom actually converted.

The reader should also bear in mind that we are describing characteristics of the group of converts rather than of individuals. On each measure a range of behavior is evidenced, but we will focus on the most common pattern. No one individual will exactly fit the entire pattern we describe. One must be careful not to overgeneralize any finding. For example, if we say, as we will, that converts do not view Jesus as divine or as a member of a trinity, still a few do (2 percent or seven people in our case). From time to time, we will point out variant categories, but mostly we will describe the normative (usual) pattern. The tables provide the reader with details for thought beyond our discussion, which is why we will have many tables in this and the next chapter.

---

1. A copy of any of the questionnaires is available from Dr. Forster upon request.

PATTERNS IN CONVERT BACKGROUNDS, BELIEFS, AND PRACTICES

Before we begin our discussion of findings from our study, we need to recall the major issues to which the study data can add insights. As we look at the specifics of the information on this group, we should keep in mind our major concerns summarized in Figure 3.2.

The religious issues focus our attention on questions of knowl-

FIGURE 3.2
SUMMARY CONCERNS ADDRESSABLE WITH STUDY DATA

Religious

- —How is motive, especially the desire to marry, involved in the effects of conversion?
- —What traditions in Judaism does the convert know and, more importantly, personally accept?
- —What is the level of religious practice of converts?
- —How strong is their commitment to Judaism compared with the practice of the Jewish community, especially of religiously identified born Jews?
- —What effects do converts have on the sanctification of the Jewish home?
- —How much do converts import Christian or pagan practices?
- —What effect does dissimilar religious backgrounds have on the marriage and on the Jewish partner?

Ethnic/Peoplehood

- —How well does the convert integrate into the Jewish community, especially with friendships and with relative relationships?
- —How well does the convert identify with important historical events for Jewish people—the Exodus, Mt. Sinai, the Holocaust, the establishment of the State of Israel?
- —How well does the convert identify with Jewish issues such as Zionism, anti-Semitism, church-state separation, responsibility for world Jewry, assimilation, and intermarriage?
- —To what extent do converts support Jewish causes and organizations by membership, donations, and volunteer work?
- —To what extent do converts identify and involve themselves in Jewish culture such as religious and/or secular Jewish art, music, literature, and events?
- —To what extent does the convert attain a personal identity as a Jew, speaking of "we" when describing Jews or Judaism?
- —To what extent do converts seek to pass a Jewish identity on to their children?

edge, beliefs, practices, and potential effects of worship and ritual-oriented endeavors of converts. The ethnic or peoplehood concerns focus our attention on questions of involvement and identification with Jews, Jewish issues, and Jewish culture. While it is listed under Ethnic Concerns, in fact, the issue of the Jewish socialization of the children of converts will stand alone as a third major area of concern. Without Jewish identified and involved children, the couple will do little to assure the continuation of the Jewish people. We will return to a discussion of these issues in Chapter 5. We now turn our attention to the specific findings of the study.

We will begin our discussion of convert situations with a look at the major patterns characterizing these converts to Judaism. The details are provided in the tables, so our discussion will summarize the main conclusions that the details suggest. Here we are only concerning ourselves with the convert data to get a "feel" for the main patterns. However, we will not be able to fully assess the meaning of these patterns until we compare convert beliefs and practices with those of born Jews. That comparison is the topic of Chapter 4. In this chapter, after we look at convert patterns, we will turn our attention to determining important relationships among these complex components. In our discussion we will group the sets of aspects we measured into PUSH, PULL, Intervening, and Outcome categories. The background variables represent potential PUSHes toward Judaism from a sympathetic home environment and PULLs from positive contacts with Jews, especially the partner and partner's family; the Intervening forces are experiences during the study period; and the Outcome is the resultant religious, ethnic, and child-rearing practices. Our conceptual model is as follows:

PUSH	PULL	INTERVEN-ING	OUTCOME
Convert family background characteristics	Convert connections to the Jewish community	Study experiences, Beliefs, Knowledge	Practices: Religious, Ethnic; Child-rearing Importance

Patterns in Convert Backgrounds

General background information on the 407 persons who finished the Introduction to Judaism course and returned our questionnaire is provided in Table 3.2. Almost half had completed the course within the past four years. Three-fourths are females whose age tended to be early thirties. Only 7 percent are minority members. They are well educated; 85 percent have at least a college education; one-third have graduate educations. They work in middle-class occupations[2] (81 percent) and have substantial household incomes ($30,000 or higher per year).

They come from well-educated, middle-class families. About 40 percent have fathers *and* mothers who have gone beyond a high school education; 60 percent of their fathers hold middle-class jobs; 12 percent of their fathers are professionals. While 60 percent of their mothers are full-time homemakers, the remaining third hold middle-class jobs. Eighty-three percent come from intact families. They tend to have one brother and one sister and to be either the oldest or second child in their families.

Since Jews tend to come from middle-class, well-educated, affluent backgrounds, it makes sense that their partners would share these characteristics. On these variables, the students who convert and those who do not convert are the same.

Patterns in Convert Background PUSH Factors

One way to make sense of the many background variables that have been found to be associated with conversion to Judaism and that we measured is to consider them as PUSH and PULL influences. The PUSH variables are those that "push" the individuals toward acceptance of diversity in general and toward a positive view of Jews and of Judaism in particular. The PULL influences are strong attracting forces from the Jewish community that "pull" the individual toward Jews and Judaism. In this section, we shall examine the PUSH variable patterns for those former students who actually converted; in the next section, we will examine the PULL factors.

As Table 3.3 shows, there are several categories representing the PUSH factors. The individual's relationship to her or his family, especially to parents, has repeatedly been found to be a factor in whether a person tends to adhere to his or her family pattern or whether the individual feels free, perhaps even compelled, to reject that family pattern and choose another, in this case largely to

---

2. Middle-class occupations include white-collar, human service, business, and professional jobs.

TABLE 3.2
MAJOR PATTERNS IN FORMER STUDENTS'
GENERAL BACKGROUND

Variable	Number	Percent
Year of Study		
1973–1980	94	23%
1981–1983	120	30%
1984–1987	189	47%
Sex		
Females	317	78%
Males	90	22%
Age		
Range: 22–69		
Average: 35 Years Old		
Most Common: 31 Years Old		
Race		
Caucasian	380	93%
Hispanic	8	2%
Asian	4	1%
Black (African-American)	4	0.5%
Other	9	3.5%
Education		
High School	32	8%
Technical	18	4%
College	222	55%
Graduate or Professional School	123	30%
Other	11	3%
Occupation		
Student	14	3%
Blue-Collar	65	16%
White-Collar/Service	124	31%
Business	81	20%
Professional	47	12%
Other	75	18%
Income of Household		
$30,000–49,999	110	28%
$50,000–75,000	113	29%
Above $75,000	110	28%

TABLE 3.3
MAJOR PATTERNS IN CONVERT BACKGROUND
PUSH FACTORS

Variable*	Number	Percent
Adolescent Relationship to Father		
Strained	115	38%
Basically Good	185	62%
Adolescent Relationship to Mother		
Strained	86	27%
Basically Good	229	73%
Father Had Jewish Friends		
None	67	26%
Some	128	49%
Many	19	7%
No Information	49	18%
Mother Had Jewish Friends		
None	72	28%
Some	135	52%
Many	16	6%
No Information	38	14%
Father's View of Jews		
Negative	48	16%
Neutral	60	20%
Positive	62	20%
No Information	134	44%
Mother's View of Jews		
Negative	36	12%
Neutral	60	19%
Positive	73	23%
No Information	146	46%
Own Political View		
Basically Conservative	48	15%
Moderate	118	37%
Basically Liberal	154	48%
Father's Religious Identification		
None	81	20%
Catholic	151	38%
Mainline Protestant	109	27%
Fundamentalist	18	5%
Other	42	10%

Mother's Religious Identification

None	34	8%
Catholic	171	42%
Mainline Protestant	137	34%
Fundamentalist	31	8%
Other	33	8%

Personal Religious Participation

None	15	5%
Little	131	46%
Regular	173	54%

Years of Formal Religious Instruction
Most Frequent: 12 Years

Baptized

No	30	9%
Yes	283	88%
Uncertain	9	3%

Confirmed

No	109	34%
Yes	207	65%

Dissatisfaction with Own Religion Before Study of
Judaism (about 10% no religion)

Dissatisfied	156	57%
Neutral	77	28%
Satisfied	39	14%

Certainty of God's Existence

Don't Believe God Exists	8	3%
Uncertain Whether God Exists	159	50%
Certain God Exists	155	47%

Adolescent View About Jesus

Doubt His Existence	37	12%
A Great Teacher	63	20%
Best of Humans	43	14%
Called by God	63	20%
Divine	104	34%

Adult View About Jesus

Doubt His Existence	46	16%
A Great Teacher	168	57%
Best of Humans	39	13%
Called by God	35	12%
Divine	7	2%

*Categories are collapsed with the negative and positive categories containing both "somewhat" and "strongly so" responses.

choose Judaism over a Christian (40 percent Catholic, 40 percent Protestant) identification and practice.

Previous studies indicate that attitudes of gentiles including parents toward Jews and toward intermarriage with Jews has changed from largely negative to overwhelmingly positive. In 1940, 60 percent of gentiles opposed intermarriage with Jews; in 1980, 80 percent approved (Mayer, 1985, p. 10). Vatican II in the Catholic community initiated a redefinition of Judaism so that a Jew could marry a Catholic without converting to Catholicism or pledging to raise the children as Catholics.

Generally, Christians are less opposed to interdating and intermarriage than are Jews. Opposition to interdating by Christian fathers (16 percent) and mothers (19 percent) is considerably lower than that of Jewish fathers (43 percent) and mothers (50 percent), and only a slightly higher percentage of Christian fathers (29 percent) and mothers (33 percent) oppose intermarriage. The majority of Jewish parents oppose intermarriage (fathers 59 percent, mothers 62 percent) (Mayer, 1985, p. 117). In all cases, the mother is more opposed than the father. Interestingly, when the gentile partner converts to Judaism, the Christian parents tend to be more accepting of the Jewish partner (fathers 44 percent, mothers 59 percent) than when their child does not convert (fathers 37 percent, mothers 56 percent) (Mayer, 1987, p. 12). Here the Christian mother is more accepting of the Jewish spouse than is the Christian father. This suggests that in deciding about conversion, gentile partners are influenced by their parents' attitudes toward Jews.

For our group, two-thirds had good relationships with their fathers, three-quarters with their mothers. (Approximately 6 percent had no contact with their fathers, 2 percent none with their mothers.) Seventy-five percent had parents who had contact with Jewish persons, and more than half of the converts' parents had Jewish friends. As a result, the converts generally were given either neutral or positive views about Jews from their parents (about 20 percent positive, two-thirds neutral or none, and 14 percent negative parental views). Politically, the converts see themselves as being more liberal than their parents. Almost half say they take liberal views on social issues, while they indicate that only about 20 percent of their parents are liberal. Liberals tend to be more accepting of social diversity and heterogeneity than do conservatives or moderates.

These converts do evidence a strong religious commitment and involvement prior to study of Judaism. Their parents tend to be fairly religiously active, attending religious services regularly (fathers 40 percent, mothers 56 percent) and engaging in home religious rituals like prayer and Bible reading (fathers 50 percent, mothers 60 percent). About half of the parents were viewed as being religiously strict in beliefs. Half (54 percent) of the converts themselves participated regularly in religious services, two-thirds were confirmed, and about half (47 percent) are certain of God's existence. Most had at least seven years of formal religious instruction as they grew up. In spite of their involvement in Christianity as adults, 57 percent indicated that they were dissatisfied with their religion. And many of them did not accept a dogmatic view of Jesus as divine and coequal with God, a view only a third of them said they had accepted as youths. They knew very little about other religions; 90 percent were uninformed of beliefs outside their own faith.

Thus, it would seem that while these converts were not driven out by negative parental relationships, their family's positive regard for and involvement with Jews, their own liberal social views, and their high regard for religious involvement but dissatisfaction with some aspects of Christianity were factors that pushed them toward Jews and Judaism. A caution is necessary here, however. We are basing our conclusion on information given us by persons who had converted to Judaism. We do not have measures on these variables prior to their involvement with a Jewish partner. Therefore, especially the religious dissatisfaction factor must be viewed with caution. For most of these converts, if they were dissatisfied with their religion, that dissatisfaction was not serious enough for them to seek an alternative religion on their own. It may just as well be that their attraction to a Jewish partner led them to consider Judaism, then to question their former religion, and then to discover sufficient dissatisfaction to justify their converting.

Patterns in Convert Background PULL Factors

The PULL factors are presented in three tables (Tables, 3.4, 3.5, and 3.6). The variables on Table 3.4 represent friendship, marital, and familial attractions. While most converts (60 percent) did not have Jewish friends during adolescence, 93 percent had Jewish friends as adults, they became seriously involved with a Jewish partner (91 percent), and found family ties with Jewish in-laws (or prospective in-laws) to be as close as (33 percent) or closer than (46 percent) their own family relationships.

TABLE 3.4
MAJOR PATTERNS IN CONVERT BACKGROUND JEWISH
CONTACT PULL FACTORS

Variable	Number	Percent
Jewish Friends as Adolescent		
None	187	62%
Some	97	31%
Many	29	9%
Percentage of Jewish Friends at Time of Study		
None	21	7%
10% or Fewer	96	30%
11%–35%	74	24%
36%–60%	74	24%
More than 60%	49	15%
Relationship with Jewish Partner at Time of Study		
Unattached	27	9%
Seriously Dating	45	14%
Planning Marriage	135	42%
Married	82	26%
Other	26	9%
Current Relationship with Jew		
Unattached	26	8%
Seriously Dating	6	2%
Planning Marriage	10	3%
Married	274	87%
Jewish Partner's Family Relationships Compared with Own		
Not as Close	63	21%
Same	98	33%
Closer	135	46%

Further PUSH and PULL influences were exerted by both sets of potential relatives once the partners became involved. Table 3.5 presents these influences. Only 25 percent of the fathers and 27 percent of the mothers of these converts were opposed to their marriage to a Jew; 89 percent of their own friends either approved of or were neutral about the intermarriage. Only about a third of the Jewish partners or parents opposed the intermarriage. However, these answers may be misleading, since the wording failed to specify parental reaction to intermarriage without conversion as the condi-

TABLE 3.5
MAJOR PATTERNS IN JEWISH PARTNER AND RELATIVE PUSH AND PULL INFLUENCES

Variable*	Number	Percent
Own Father's Reaction to Intermarriage		
Disapproval	46	25%
Neutral	61	32%
Approval	81	43%
Own Mother's Reaction to Intermarriage		
Disapproval	62	27%
Neutral	52	22%
Approval	120	51%
Own Friend's Reaction to Jewish Partner		
Disapproval	28	11%
Neutral	36	14%
Approval	192	75%
Partner's Father's Reaction to Intermarriage		
Disapproval	79	36%
Neutral	22	10%
Approval	117	54%
Partner's Mother's Reaction to Intermarriage		
Disapproval	93	38%
Neutral	22	9%
Approval	128	53%
Partner's Friend's Reaction to Intermarriage		
Disapproval	27	11%
Neutral	35	14%
Approval	184	75%
Own Father's Reaction to Potential Conversion		
Disapproval	63	32%
Neutral	62	31%
Approval	77	37%
Own Mother's Reaction to Potential Conversion		
Disapproval	90	35%
Neutral	61	24%
Approval	107	41%
Partner's Father's Reaction to Potential Conversion		
Disapproval	13	6%
Neutral	24	12%
Approval	171	82%

Partner's Mother's Reaction to Potential Conversion

Disapproval	14	6%
Neutral	18	8%
Approval	203	86%

Partner's Religious Activity

Not Active	57	21%
Some	165	62%
Regular	46	17%

*Categories are collapsed with the negative and positive categories containing both "somewhat" and "strongly so" responses.

tion. Had the question been clearer, the negative reactions of Jewish parents to a nonconvert intermarriage might have been higher. The Jewish partner's friends were supportive of the intermarriage (89 percent positive or neutral). There was little parental resistance to conversion (only a third of the converts' parents opposed conversion; 6 percent of the Jewish partners' parents did so).

The PULL factor that our data indicates as being the strongest is that of the partner. Three-fourths of the Jewish partners maintained some religious practices (17 percent were regularly active); according to the converts, 85 percent of the partners felt that maintaining their own Jewish identity was important, and of that group, 61 percent felt their Jewish identity was *very* important. While 53 percent of the converts were glad their partner was a Jew, only 2 percent of the Jewish partners were perceived to be happy with their partners' not being a Jew, 20 percent were perceived to be unhappy about the situation, and 37 percent were perceived to be ambivalent. The Jewish partners came from homes where more than 80 percent of their parents were religious; 22 percent of the partners' fathers and 17 percent of the partners' mothers were perceived to be very religious. While the Jewish partner tended not to be involved with Jewish organizations (54 percent were not, a pattern typical of young professional Jews), more than half had 60 percent or more of their friends as Jews.

In sum, the Jewish partner seems to exert a strong pull toward Judaism because of his or her personal commitment and involvement. However, it is not necessarily for religious reasons that the Jewish partner wishes to maintain a Jewish identity. Discussions with Jewish partners indicate a more tribal or ethnic connection than a religious one. Jewish partners often say that they can't see themselves fitting in the gentile community, and therefore they desire to retain their sense of belonging to the Jewish community, a sense of belonging retained and enhanced by having their partner more Jewishly involved and accepted. Friend and parental influences seem largely supportive of both intermarriage and of conversion. While we should not forget that a significant minority of these converts faced obstacles to their involvement in Judaism, the majority did not.

Reasons for Interest in Conversion of Gentile Partners

Anyone who wants to become a Jew must either be insincere or unbalanced (Eichhorn, 1965, p. 86).

The Jewish community as a whole still evidences great suspicion toward converts. The belief seems to be that no one would freely choose to be a Jew, to subject themselves to anti-Semitism, to take on the burden of *halacha,* so converts must be insincere and a subversive element. Since Jews know of their own Marranos who faked being Christians for centuries, they have historical grounds for being suspicious. Sincere converts to Judaism today are not in danger of their lives if they convert, and there are compelling yet suspicious social and personal reasons for them to go through the conversion process as we have just indicated.

Figure 3.3 lists various reasons for conversion attributed to converts. We have added to the list factors that our experience suggests are important also. We have divided the reasons into four general categories: (1) Religious related, (2) Marriage related, (3) Community related, and (4) Personal related. Only the first category, religious related, is considered legitimate in the traditional Jewish view. In fact, rabbis are not to convert anyone who comes for other than religious reasons. However, the majority of conversions occur in the context of an impending marriage (40 percent) or child (22 percent) (Mayer and Sheingold, 1979, p. 21, and our data).

Even those 15 percent who convert before meeting their Jewish partner find themselves suspect in the Jewish community. To Jews, the prototype of a convert is Ruth. (Interestingly to us, anyway, Jews do not seem to really deal with the fact that Ruth, a Moabite, married a Jew, Naomi's son, long before she "converted.") Nor do Jews tend to differentiate among converts. It is assumed by those of a negative bent, even when the facts are known to be otherwise,

FIGURE 3.3
SUMMARY OF REASONS PROPOSED TO EXPLAIN GENTILE CONVERSION TO JUDAISM

Religious Related

—Believed Judaism a superior religion
—Identified with Jesus as a Jew
—Felt God leading
—Felt Jewish beliefs made sense
—Liked Jewish worship
—Liked the realism in Jewish routine practices
—Searched for better religious identity
—Sense of spiritual or religious need
—Serious personal event caused questioning of faith

Marriage Related

—Concern for religious identity of children
—Desire for a Jewish wedding
—Desire to provide children with a coherent family tradition and religion
—To avoid dissonance in the home
—To please the Jewish in-laws
—To please the Jewish partner
—To share faith and practice with partner

Community Related

—Admiration of Jewish accomplishments in the face of hostilities
—Desire to belong to a close community
—Desire to be part of an ancient heritage that has withstood the test of time
—Felt Jews lived better lives than Christians
—Had many Jewish friends
—Identification with the Jewish fate
—To be part of a Jewish social millieu

Personal Related

—Belief that there will be material or status gain ("all Jews are rich and powerful")
—Excitement of a new and different group and religion
—Forbidden fruit attraction
—Rebellion against parents

that all converts are suspect, having converted for utilitarian reasons.

While Mayer and Sheingold used only four categories of reasons
for conversions, their findings show that 32.2 percent of gentiles
converted out of personal conviction, 38 percent for the sake of the
mate or relatives, 8.9 percent for the sake of children, and 20.9
percent for a combination of reasons (1979, p. 21). By these measures, at least one-third of the converts embraced Judaism out of
conviction. Religious conviction reasons include fulfillment of a
spiritual need/search, agreement with Jewish beliefs and perspectives, liking/benefiting from concrete Jewish worship experiences,
and a spiritual "calling" or "leading."

According to Mayer and Sheingold, 47 percent of converts become
so for marriage-related reasons (for the sake of mate, in-laws, and/
or children). However, these categories do not necessarily themselves indicate that such family motives for conversion cannot
produce genuine adherence. In a recent study of converts, Mayer
found as we did that converts tended to have more religiously
oriented spouses and in-laws, to have a stronger sense of the need
for a religious identity and experience, and to share in communal
attitudes and involvements (1987). Mayer's 1987 data, like ours,
show that converts to Judaism tended to have very or moderately
religious spouses (66.7 percent), fathers-in-law (66 percent), and
mothers-in-law (60 percent); nonconverts showed 25.1 percent, 39.4
percent, and 39.1 percent respectively. Mayer's data also indicate
that the spouses of converts were more unhappy about their mates
not being Jewish (40.6 percent of Jews unhappy that partner is a
gentile to 14.4 percent of gentiles unhappy with a Jew, a somewhat
higher rate than our group), while converts were themselves more
happy to have gotten a Jewish mate (54.6 percent of converts happy
having a Jewish partner to 30.2 percent Jews happy with a partner
of gentile background). Mayer also found that persons were likely
to convert if requested to do so by their future in-laws. Certainly
there should be concern that persons are not permitted to rush into
converting to Judaism for expediency; but it may well be that
conversion primarily for family reasons can still be genuine.

Persons who are primarily connected to the Jewish community
and ethnic heritage are not likely to convert to Judaism. They are
more likely to just participate actively in the Jewish community.
However, since it is likely that persons convert for a variety of
reasons, not just one, attachment to the community, as in Ruth's

case, may be a binding or strengthening force (for example, see Helfgott, 1987). Since becoming a Jew requires both a religious and an ethnic involvement and identity, community relatedness should be a positive indicator of attachment.

The personal related factors for conversion seem the least mature and, therefore, most suspect. However, Mayer's study and our own indicate that converts are not more distant from their fathers than nonconverts (in Mayer's data 36 percent of converts express distance versus 41 percent of nonconverts) and only slightly more distant from their mothers (34 percent of converts express distance versus 29 percent of nonconverts) (1987). Information on the other factors is not currently available.

The Jewish community is suspicious of the reasons gentiles convert to Judaism especially when the conversion occurs in the context of an impending marriage. There is also the fear that even if the person converts for purely religious reasons, as Rosenthal stated, the conversion may still be a meaningless, external ritual and, in addition, the deep prior cultural and religious conditioning may win out eventually anyway (1963, p. 7).

With this background to Jewish concerns about the reasons for conversion, what does our data show? From our converts' point of view, the factors exercising the most influence on their decision to study Judaism with conversion a strong possibility are shown in Table 3.6. The top five attraction forces for these converts were:

- See Jewish beliefs as sensible
- Desire to share in Jewish partner's faith
- Desire to be able to provide coherent, consistent family traditions
- Belief that Judaism is an answer to their own religious search
- Desire to marry a Jew

While only the first and fourth are valid reasons for conversion in the viewpoint of traditional rabbis, most converts had six or seven reasons attracting them to Judaism; a quarter identified ten or more reasons. However, when asked to identify the one main influence, most chose wanting to marry a Jew. It remains to be seen whether marital reasons lead to worse outcomes for Jewish practice than do religious reasons.

Most converts (82 percent) felt they were themselves the prime

TABLE 3.6
MAJOR PATTERNS IN ATTRACTIONS (PULL) TO JUDAISM

Variable	Number	Percent
Factors for Original Interest*		
Sensible Jewish Beliefs	201	63%
Share Faith of Partner	195	62%
Provide Coherent Family Traditions	191	60%
Jewish Friends	156	51%
Wanted to Marry a Jew	154	49%
Answer to a Religious Search	147	46%
Concern about Children's Religious Identity	147	46%
Read about Judaism	142	45%
Spiritual Need	121	38%
Realism of Judaism	113	36%
Admire Jews' Survival	92	29%
Desire to Belong to a Close Community	84	27%
Ancient Heritage	77	24%
Liked Jewish Worship	68	22%
God's Leading	34	11%
Serious Personal Questioning	28	9%
Excitement of New Religion	24	8%
Identified with Jesus as Jew	19	6%
Liked Jewish Lives	11	4%
Most Important Influence (Top 4)		
Wanted to Marry a Jew	56	18%
Provide Coherent Family Traditions	43	14%
Share Faith of Partner	42	14%
Sensible Jewish Beliefs	39	13%
Second Most Important Influence (Top 4)		
Provide Coherent Family Traditions	65	21%
Share Faith of Partner	52	17%
Sensible Jewish Beliefs	46	15%
Answer to Religious Search	24	8%
Primary Initiator of Conversion Consideration**		
Self	261	82%
Partner	140	44%
Partner's Mother	33	10%
Partner's Father	27	9%
A Rabbi	22	7%
Other	16	5%
A Friend	12	4%

*Respondents could choose more than one reason so percents represent those who chose each factor. Listed most to least frequently chosen reason attracted to Judaism.

**Respondents could choose more than one reason so percents represent those who chose each factor.

initiator of the decision to consider conversion to Judaism; 44 percent indicated recognition of their partner's role.

Patterns in Study Experiences and Conversion Reasons

If we envision conversion and its practice patterns as the outcome and family, friend, and partner influences as pushing and pulling forces, the period of study may be viewed as intervening between input (PUSH and PULL) and output (conversion practices). Table 3.7 presents data on the study events.

Most of our group indicated a rather short period of formal study before deciding about conversion. Eighty-five percent studied less than two years, three-quarters less than a year. However, three-quarters had attended some synagogue services before beginning study, one quarter attended regularly, and 87 percent liked Jewish worship in comparison with their own. During the time of study, 58 percent attended services regularly, 95 percent at least some. Two-thirds got involved in the Jewish community through lectures, films, social groups, and so on.

Another aspect that intervenes is the responses the potential converts received during the time of study. These responses are summarized in Table 3.8. Two-thirds of the converts experienced positive responses from the Jewish community. Only 14 percent encountered blatantly negative responses from Jews, but even those negative responses usually occurred only occasionally (56 percent). Gentile friends, their mother, and a rabbi were the usual sources of discouragement to conversion. Those students (14 percent) who decided not to convert to Judaism felt they would be accepted by Jews anyway and were deterred by personal and religious considerations. Most made their decision in their late twenties. The most important reasons for the actual conversion were:

- Concern about their children's religious upbringing
- Positive effects of Judaism on their own religious life
- Marriage to a Jew
- Positive regard for Jewish beliefs

Here, as with reasons to study Judaism, religious as well as family/marriage reasons are paramount.

TABLE 3.7
MAJOR PATTERNS IN STUDY EXPERIENCES AS
POTENTIAL CONVERT (INTERVENING)

Variable*	Number	Percent
Prior Synagogue Attendance		
Never	74	23%
A Few Times	174	54%
Regularly	72	23%
Comparison of Jewish Worship with Own Religion		
Dislike	23	8%
Neutral	13	5%
Like	247	87%
Studying Beyond Course**		
Talk with Jewish Partner	190	59%
Talk with Jewish Friends	178	55%
With Rabbi	158	49%
Other Study	95	29%
Lectures on Judaism	91	28%
Formal Courses	41	13%
Synagogue Participation During Study		
None	16	5%
Some	120	37%
Regular	187	58%
Participation in Jewish Community Activities During Study		
None	103	32%
Some	153	47%
Regular	67	21%

*Categories are collapsed with the negative and positive categories containing both "somewhat" and "strongly so" responses.
**Listed from most to least frequent.

Patterns in Effects of Conversion

Table 3.9 gives information about the personal, familial, partner, and religious effects of conversion. Only 15 percent converted before they met a Jewish partner; 58 percent converted before marriage but after serious involvement with a Jew; 18 percent converted before the birth of their child in a mixed marriage. Our data again are similar to Mayer's data that we cited previously. Two-thirds indicated that the decision about whether or not to convert was easy

TABLE 3.8
MAJOR PATTERNS IN REACTION TO
POTENTIAL CONVERSION

Variable	Number	Percent
Acceptance by Jewish Community*		
Negative	41	14%
Neutral	47	15%
Positive	214	61%
Frequency of Negative Response from Jews		
Never	134	42%
Occasionally	117	56%
Frequently	8	2%
Ease to Feel Belong with Jewish People*		
Difficult	102	32%
Neutral	26	8%
Easy	194	60%
Source of Discouragement for Conversion**		
Other	68	31%
Non-Jewish Friends	59	27%
Own Mother	51	23%
Rabbi	48	22%
Own Relatives	43	20%
Own Father	29	13%
Jewish Friends	20	9%
Partner	18	8%
Jewish People	18	8%
Partner's Mother	12	6%
Partner's Father	9	4%
Reasons Not to Convert**		
Can Have a Jewish-Oriented Home without Conversion	26	41%
Don't Need to Convert to Belong	26	41%
Other Personal Reasons	24	38%
Religion Not Important	17	27%
Against Religious Beliefs	14	22%
No Positive Religious Effect	13	21%
Didn't Like Being a Jew	10	16%
Partner Opposed	8	13%
Concern about Family	6	10%
Concern about Anti-Semisitm	5	8%
Jewish Opposition	4	6%

Concern about Reactions of Non-Jews	4	6%
Too Difficult	2	3%
Family Opposition	2	3%
Most Important Reasons Not to Convert		
Other Personal Reasons	19	32%
Can Have Jewish-Oriented Home without Conversion	12	25%
Against Own Religious Beliefs	9	15%
Religion Not Important	7	12%
Reasons to Convert**		
Concern about Children	207	63%
Like Jewish Beliefs	201	61%
Positive Effect on Religious Life	189	57%
Like Jewish Religious Practices	175	53%
To Marry a Jew	170	51%
To Belong to the Jewish Community	131	40%
Identification with the Jewish Experience	115	35%
To Please Jewish In-laws	68	21%
Acceptance by Jews	59	18%
Pressure from Partner	44	13%
Other	18	6%
Most Important Reasons To Convert		
Concern about Children	78	24%
Positive Effect on Religious Life	75	23%
To Marry a Jew	60	18%
Like Jewish Beliefs	53	16%

*Categories are collapsed with the negative and positive categories containing both "somewhat" and "strongly so" responses.

**Respondents could choose more than one reason so percents represent those who chose each factor. Listed most to least frequent.

to make. After actually converting, half initially had doubts about their decision, but only one-third continued to have doubts, usually on an an infrequent basis. Their most important doubts were:

- Being able to give up former religious practices
- Being accepted by Jews
- Being able to relate to relatives
- Being able to handle discrimination

Conversion brought some change to the converts' life. Eighty-nine percent changed their life-style (16 percent made major life-style

TABLE 3.9
MAJOR PATTERNS OF EFFECTS OF CONVERSION

Variable	Number	Percent
Doubts about Conversion		
No Doubts	162	59%
Some Doubts	145	44%
Serious Doubts	20	6%
Frequency of Doubts about Conversion Currently		
Never	224	69%
Occasionally	93	28%
Frequently	11	3%
Reason for Doubts about Conversion*		
Giving Up Former Religious Practices	102	38%
Being Accepted by Jews	83	31%
Relating to Relatives	58	22%
Handling Discrimination	52	20%
Disappointment with Jews	29	11%
Fear at Rejecting Jesus	24	9%
Other	24	9%
Relating to Former Friends	23	9%
Concern about Salvation	22	8%
Change in Life-style Because of Conversion**		
None	35	11%
Some	230	73%
Major	51	16%
Change in Religious Beliefs		
None	16	5%
Some	203	64%
Major	97	31%
Importance of Religion as a Result of Studies**		
Against Religion	1	0%
Religion Unimportant	7	2%
Religion Some Importance	181	60%
Religion Very Important	114	38%
Increased Practice Factors Since Study*		
Knowledge of Judaism	279	87%
Commitment to Jewish People	246	77%
Practice of Judaism	234	74%
Involvement with Jews	110	66%

Importance of Jewish Identity**

Not Important or Unsure	78	24%
Somewhat Important	111	35%
Very Important	129	41%

Own Father's Acceptance of Conversion**

Negative	21	10%
Neutral	62	31%
Ambivalent	42	21%
Positive	77	38%

Own Mother's Acceptance of Conversion**

Negative	32	13%
Neutral	61	24%
Ambivalent	58	22%
Positive	107	41%

Negative Effects of Conversion on Relationships**

With Christian Relatives	49	16%
With Christian Friends	26	8%
With Own Mother	21	7%
With Own Father	19	7%
With partner	10	3%
With Jewish Friends	6	2%
With Jewish Relatives	4	1%
With Jews in General	4	1%

Positive Effects of Conversion on Relationships**

With Partner	144	47%
With Jews in General	139	45%
With Jewish Relatives	116	40%
With Jewish Friends	91	29%
With Own Father	49	18%
With Own Mother	21	7%
With Christian Relatives	10	3%
With Christian Friends	1	1%

Get Along with Partner's Father Versus Own

Not As Well	44	21%
As Well	99	49%
Better	60	30%

Get Along with Partner's Mother Versus Own

Not As Well	69	29%
As Well	105	45%
Better	61	26%

Frequency of Contact with Jewish Versus Non-Jewish
Friends

Non-Jews More	48	17%
About Equal	141	49%
Jews More	100	34%

Disagreements with Partner Because of Different
Backgrounds**

None	146	51%
Some	132	46%
Many	9	3%

Helpfulness of Introductory Course**

For Understanding Jewish Beliefs	306	96%
For Understanding Jewish Obligations	300	94%
For Conversion Decision	288	90%
For Gaining Practice Skills	235	73%
For Information about Jewish Resources	167	52%

Perception of Contribution of Converts to Judaism**

A Negative Influence	1	1%
No Difference	36	11%
A Positive Influence	276	88%

Perception of Convert Observance Versus Born Jews**

Less Observant	22	7%
Equally Observant	112	35%
More Observant	177	58%

Perception of Convert Participation Versus Born
Jews**

Less Active	64	21%
Equally Active	158	51%
More Active	85	28%

*Respondents could choose more than one reason so percents represent those who chose each factor.
**Categories are collapsed with the negative and positive categories containing both "somewhat" and "strongly so" responses.

changes); 95 percent had changes in their religious beliefs (31 percent had major belief changes), and religion tended to become more important to them. Their knowledge of Judaism, commitment to Jews, and involvement with Jews increased. They felt it important to be identified as a Jew (76 percent, with 41 percent very important).

Their conversion was basically accepted by their parents. Only 10 percent of the fathers and 13 percent of the mothers expressed negative concerns about their action. Some negative effects on relationships with Christian relatives (16 percent) or Christian friends (8 percent) were experienced, but these negative relational effects were offset by positive effects on their relationship with their partner (47 percent), Jews in general (45 percent), Jewish relatives (40 percent), and Jewish friends (29 percent). Most found they got along with their Jewish relatives as well as or better than their own parents (79 percent related well with their Jewish father-in-law, 71 percent with their Jewish mother-in-law); about 30 percent found a better relationship with their Jewish in-laws than with their own families. Their involvement with Jewish friends was equal to (49 percent) or more than (34 percent) their relationships with gentiles. And finally, most (51 percent) found little disagreement over religious matters with their partner.

The converts found the Introduction to Judaism course particularly helpful in gaining understanding of Jewish beliefs and obligations, though less so for actually developing needed skills or for learning about Jewish community resources. Eighty percent or more believed that converts are a positive influence on Judaism and that they are equally as observant and involved as born Jews. Fifty-eight percent felt converts were actually more observant than born Jews, though only 28 percent thought converts were more active.

In all, the effects of conversion appear to be positive as reported by these converts. They encountered significantly positive effects on their relationships with Jews including their partner and in-laws as their life-styles and religious beliefs changed.

Patterns in Beliefs of Converts

We now turn our attention to the specific religious and ethnic beliefs articulated by these converts (Table 3.10). Our final assessment of the meaning of these belief patterns will be deferred to the next chapter where we will compare these patterns with born Jews.

The general religious belief patterns indicate that converts are religiously oriented. They tend to believe in God (61 percent) and feel close to Him (66 percent); they have direct experience of the Divine (54 percent) and are religiously concerned.

While 85 percent can honestly affirm the *Shema* (Hear, O Israel, the Lord, Our God, is One), except for a belief that humans can

TABLE 3.10
MAJOR PATTERNS OF BELIEFS AGREEMENT

Variable*	Number	Percent
General Religious Beliefs		
Frequently Feel Close to God	106	66%
Believe in God as Father	203	61%
Prayer Is Important	190	60%
Religion Influences Daily Life	109	34%
Experience Presence of Divine in Life	172	54%
Often Talk about Religion	143	45%
Jewish Religious Beliefs		
Humans Have Free Will to Choose Good	302	97%
There Is Only One God	268	85%
Judaism Has More Truth than Other Religions	258	82%
Jews Have a Covenantal Relationship with God	235	74%
Rabbinic Interpretations Are Valid	215	63%
Beliefs Don't Matter, A Moral Life Does	190	60%
God Promised the Land of Israel to the Jews	196	63%
The Hebrew Bible Is God's Revealed Word	177	56%
Jesus' Messiahship Was a Creation of the Early Church	154	50%
Jews Are Chosen to Be a Light to the Nations	121	39%
Moral Non-Jews Will Be Saved	90	29%
God Will Send the Messiah at Time's End	73	24%
Christian Religious Beliefs		
Jesus Broke with Judaism	58	19%
God Revealed Himself in Jesus	47	15%
Jesus Rose from the Dead	34	11%
God Exists as a Trinity	33	11%
Jesus Will Return as Messiah	19	6%
The Resurrection Proves Jesus was the Messiah	17	5%
Jewish Ethnic Beliefs		
There Must Always Be Jewish People	302	97%
Anti-Semitism Is a Problem in the U.S.	291	92%
Having Satisfying Life Goals	280	90%
Being Jewish Is Personally Important	271	87%
Feel Comfortable in Jewish Settings	269	86%
Feel Obliged to Help World Jewry	256	81%
Want to Be Part of the Jewish Community	253	81%
The U.S. Should Aid Israel	250	79%
Feel a Bond to Israel	225	72%

It Is Important to Vote for Politicians Who Support Israel	209	67%
The Synagogue Should Help Minorities	184	60%
The Press Is Too Negative about Israel	133	42%
Jewish Parents Should Make Sure Their Kids Don't Marry Non-Jews	76	25%

*Categories are collapsed to include "agree" and "strongly agree" responses.

choose to do good (free will over original sin—97 percent), support for major traditional Jewish beliefs is mixed. Though 74 percent believe Jews have a covenantal relationship with God, only 39 percent accept the traditional view that Jews are to be a light to the nations. Beliefs about salvation through good works and the promised Messiah are the least likely to be held. Perhaps more disturbing is the fact that about 10 percent still hold distinctly Christian religious views about the role of Jesus.

The ethnic/peoplehood concerns for this group appear fairly strong except in their lack of criticism about the attitude of the press toward Israel (58 percent not concerned) and lack of concern about the marriage partners of their children (75 percent not concerned). Otherwise, they seem to accept the importance of a Jewish presence in the world (97 percent), are concerned about anti-Semitism in the United States (92 percent), and want to support Israel (72 percent) and world Jewry (79 percent). They feel comfortable in Jewish settings (90 percent) and want to be part of the Jewish community (81 percent).

Patterns in Convert Knowledge

As a group, Jews have a commitment to learning, believing that knowledge leads to practice. How knowledgeable do these converts view themselves? Table 3.11 presents information on how knowledgeable about Jewish religious beliefs, practice requirements, history, and community resources these converts assess themselves to be. Again, we will wait with final judgment until our next chapter so we can compare these knowledge patterns with those of born Jews.

While two-thirds feel they know the Jewish view about God, only half are aware of the controversy about who is a Jew; fewer than half are informed about either the Jewish view toward Jesus (49

TABLE 3.11
MAJOR PATTERNS OF CONVERTS' PERCEIVED
JEWISH KNOWLEDGE

Variable	Good Knowledge		No Knowledge	
	Number	Percent	Number	Percent
Jewish Religious Beliefs*				
Jewish View of God	218	68%	3	1%
Controversy on Who Is a Jew	174	54%	10	3%
View of Jesus	158	49%	6	2%
View of Christianity	144	45%	6	2%
Reform Judaism	141	44%	4	1%
Conservative Judaism	111	35%	10	3%
Orthodox Judaism	84	26%	13	4%
The Talmud	72	23%	5	2%
Jewish Practice Requirements*				
Passover Seder	257	80%	1	1%
Yom Kipper Observance	238	74%	10	3%
Sabbath Observance	116	68%	1	1%
Brit Milah—Circumcision	198	61%	7	2%
Sitting Shiva—Mourning	173	55%	9	3%
Expected Mitzvot	172	54%	6	2%
Kashrut—Dietary Laws	154	48%	8	3%
Kosher Home	139	43%	7	2%
Mikvah—Family Purity	104	39%	12	4%
Sukkot	115	36%	18	6%
Daily Worship	82	26%	14	4%
Jewish History and Issues*				
Shoah (Holocaust)	251	78%	1	1%
Biblical History	146	46%	5	2%
Zionism	103	42%	9	3%
Postbiblical History	132	41%	9	3%
Jewish Community Resources**				
Spertus College of Judaica	274	86%	4	1%
Michael Reese Hospital	191	60%	5	2%
Jewish Community Centers	185	59%	7	2%
Mount Sinai Hospital	153	48%	5	2%
The Ark	141	44%	42	13%
The Sentinel	131	41%	103	32%
Jewish Vocational Service	97	31%	49	16%
Council for Jewish Elderly	93	30%	41	13%

Jewish Family and Community Services	93	30%	41	13%
Jewish Children's Bureau	75	24%	61	19%
Board of Jewish Education	55	22%	55	18%
Hebrew Theological College	55	18%	84	27%
Drexel Home	27	9%	138	44%
Associated Talmud Torahs	19	6%	144	47%
Response Center	15	5%	143	46%

*Categories collapsed to include "adequate" and "serious" knowledge responses.
**Categories are collapsed to include "somewhat" and "very familiar" responses.

percent) or toward Christianity (45 percent); and they are not very knowledgeable about the three major branches in Judaism. While 80 percent know the requirements for a Passover seder and three-quarters know the requirements for Yom Kippur and two-thirds for the Sabbath, good knowledge of other practices tends to be held by 40 percent or fewer of the group. Only 26 percent know the daily worship service.

While not especially well informed about Jewish history, three-quarters know about the Holocaust, which is a highly stressed recent event and issue in the Jewish community. Finally, except for knowing about Spertus College (86 percent), where many of the Introduction to Judaism classes were held, and Michael Reese Hospital (60 percent), other Jewish community resources are known by only a quarter to a third of this group.

We have selected fairly rigorous criteria for this table, including only those who indicated adequate or better knowledge. For reader interest, we have included the number and percentage of the converts who indicated that they had *no* knowledge about these categories. Few converts entirely lack knowledge of these topics, except that one-third are unaware of the *Sentinel,* a weekly Jewish news magazine that could keep them informed. We must also keep in mind that we have measured not actual knowledge but perceived knowledge. It may be that converts are really too tough on themselves in evaluating how much they actually know. They may be aware from their studies of how much the experts know and, therefore, feel themselves to be less knowledgeable than they are if we could test them and compare what they really know with born Jews.

Major Patterns of Religious Practices

As previously indicated, the main controversies about the role of converts for the Jewish community hinge on three areas of behavior:

(1) religious practices, (2) ethnic/community involvement, and (3) child-rearing socialization. In this section, we will examine our data on the first two areas; in the next section, we will address the third area, child-rearing.

Jewish Religious Practices

The religious practices question for converts is actually twofold. On one hand is a concern about their adherence to major religious practices that are distinctly Jewish; on the other hand is a concern about the extent of their importing Christian-oriented practices into their households. We will look at both areas.

The list of practices in Table 3.12 represents behaviors traditionally expected of Jews. Here we will compare the converts against an absolute standard; that is, the highest standard would be complete adherence (100 percent) for each of the behaviors. In the next chapter, we will compare the converts' practices against typical Conservative and Reform born Jew patterns to see how well they stack up to actual Jewish religious community norms.

Clearly Hanukah, Passover, and the High Holidays (Rosh Hashanah and Yom Kippur) are the favored rituals for participation by these converts. However, even here there are gaps in full participation. While 91 percent have a Hanukah menorah, only 82 percent actually light the candles for the holiday. While 85 percent participate in a seder, only 55 percent eat only unleavened bread during the entire eight days and only 17 percent have separate dishes. While 80 percent participate in High Holiday services, only 67 percent fast on Yom Kippur. There is a gap between knowledge of requirements and practice as shown by the fact that 65 percent know how to say the *Kiddush* (prayer over wine) but only 34 percent usually do so; 79 percent have a prayer book but only 9 percent say daily prayers, and less than 1 percent attend a *minyan*. (These latter two practices are not stressed for women, and these converts are mainly women.) What about Sabbath observance, since the Sabbath is highly stressed by the rabbis? While two-thirds belong to a synagogue, only one-third regularly attend Sabbath services; while 70 percent know the blessing for the Sabbath candles, only 47 percent actually light candles; and only 30 percent engage in any other Sabbath home rituals or prayers; an even smaller number (16 percent) try to observe the prohibition against work on the Sabbath. Finally, since this group is by their own admission not well versed in Judaism, it is distressing to see that only 17 percent engage in

TABLE 3.12
MAJOR PATTERNS OF REGULAR JEWISH
RELIGIOUS PRACTICES

Religious Practices*	Frequently		Never	
	Number	Percent	Number	Percent
Have a Hanukah menorah	291	91%	29	9%
Participate in Passover seder	270	85%	11	4%
Exchange Hanukah presents	262	83%	22	7%
Light Hanukah candles	256	82%	17	5%
Attend Yom Kippur services	256	81%	17	5%
Have a Jewish prayer book	254	79%	67	21%
Attend Rosh Hashanah services	250	79%	24	8%
Know *Shema* (in Hebrew)	246	77%	74	23%
Have a Jewish Bible	240	75%	81	25%
Have a *Mezzuzah* on outside doorway(s)	231	73%	87	27%
Know candle blessing in Hebrew	223	70%	98	30%
Belong to a synagogue	220	69%	100	31%
Fast on Yom Kippur	209	67%	51	16%
Know *Kiddush* (over wine) in Hebrew	203	63%	118	37%
Know *Hamotzi* (over bread) in Hebrew	190	59%	131	41%
East only unleavened food during Passover	173	55%	60	19%
Light Sabbath candles	149	47%	73	23%
Attend Sabbath services	114	36%	10	3%
Attend Purim services	111	35%	88	28%
Say *Kiddush* over wine (or partner)	110	34%	116	36%
Have a home Sabbath service	96	30%	110	34%
Observe Sukkot	79	25%	97	31%
Have a *Mezzuzah* on inside doorway(s)	78	25%	238	75%
Have separate Passover dishes	55	17%	265	83%
Engage in formal study of Judaism	54	17%	118	37%
Refrain from work on the Sabbath	50	16%	170	53%
Keep kosher at home	49	15%	185	58%
Eat kosher away from home	31	10%	157	49%
Say daily morning prayers	29	9%	216	67%
Have an active part in Jewish worship service	27	8%	183	57%
Use *Tefillin* (or partner)	8	3%	269	86%
Attend a daily *Minyan*	1	0%	276	87%

*Importance of Religious Activities***

Learn to follow the prayers	281	88%
Continued study of Judaism	272	88%
Learn the prayers in Hebrew	256	81%
Live near a synagogue	236	75%
Learn Hebrew	199	51%
Bar or *Bat Mitzvah*	85	27%

*Reason for Not Belonging to Synagogue***

Financial	44	19%
Other	28	12%
Lack of time	23	10%
Can't find a synagogue that feel at home in	19	8%
Lack of interest	17	8%
Just moved	16	7%
Don't like organized religion	10	4%
None close	9	4%
Never invited to join	9	4%

*Rabbi Support for Converts**

Negative	9	3%
Ambivalent	15	5%
Neutral	10	12%
Positive	245	77%

*Categories collapsed for the negative and positive categories.
**More than one choice possible.

any form of ongoing Jewish religious education through lectures, study groups, or formal classes.

From an absolute standard, then, these converts fall short on all of the measures. Their participation in the three main holidays would parallel Christian patterns of attendance at Christmas and Easter services, with the addition in Judaism of Rosh Hashanah and Yom Kippur. Nor do they seem inclined to further their knowledge. Their practice lags behind their knowledge as evidenced by the actual use of Hebrew prayers that they have learned. Few (8 percent) actively participate in synagogue services. We will leave final judgment about these practice patterns for the next chapter when we compare them with born Jews.

Again, we have selected a fairly tough standard, focusing on those who often or almost always engage in these practices. On the other end of the scale, what of those who say they never engage in these practices? The second column in Table 3.12 gives that data. While few of the converts never participate in the most popular observances and only 3 percent never attend Sabbath services, other Sabbath observances do not fare well. One-fourth never light Sabbath candles, one-third have no home Sabbath rituals, and 53 percent never refrain from work on the Sabbath. Sixty-seven percent never say the morning prayers. And 37 percent never engage in any form of Jewish education.

Table 3.12 also presents a few additional items to help our understanding of these converts' patterns of religious practice. While few converts are engaged in Jewish religious learning (17 percent, with 37 percent not at all), the majority do believe that study is important (88 percent) and want to learn the prayers (88 percent). Unfortunately, we do not have information about why these converts are not actually pursuing the learning they believe to be important. These attitudes/needs may be an opening for further outreach by the Jewish community and should be explored. They do seem to have positive regard for the synagogue; two-thirds are members, three-quarters feel it is important to live near a synagogue, and most (77 percent) feel the rabbi to be positive toward them as converts. Those who do not belong to a synagogue express problems with costs (19 percent) and time (10 percent), but few (8 percent) express lack of interest.

Christian Religious Practices

If these converts as a group are not rigorously practicing the traditional religious aspects of Judaism, are they bringing Christian practices directly into the household? Table 3.13 indicates some involvement with Christmas presents (74 percent), family gatherings (59 percent), and decorations (55 percent), but otherwise a low rate of actual religious service participation (about 5 percent). The "December dilemma" seems to be answered by involvement with relatives in family gatherings; only 10 percent have their own Christmas tree; however, a quarter do exchange Christmas presents within their own household. Attendance at Easter observances is lower, only 28 percent meeting with relatives and 3 percent going to an actual religious service. Finally, only 2 percent frequently attend Christian religious services at other times. Clearly, it is Christmas that retains the largest influence for these converts.

TABLE 3.13
MAJOR PATTERNS OF REGULAR
CHRISTIAN RELIGIOUS PRACTICES

Variable	Frequently*		Never	
	Number	Percent	Number	Percent
Exchange Christmas presents with relatives	231	74%	36	12%
Attend a Christmas family gathering	185	59%	55	18%
Decorate home at Christmas/ Hanukah holidays	173	55%	66	21%
Send Christmas cards	117	37%	113	36%
Attend Easter family gatherings	89	28%	154	49%
Exchange Christmas presents in own household	79	25%	211	67%
Decorate a Christmas tree	30	10%	259	82%
Attend a Christmas service	14	5%	264	84%
Attend Easter services	10	3%	279	88%
Attend a Christian service	6	2%	194	61%

*Categories are collapsed to include "often" and "almost always" responses.

Only about 20 percent are actually able to discontinue any involvement with the Christmas-related activities of decorating and family gatherings, and only 12 percent stop the exchange of Christmas presents. Easter holds less of an attraction; half never attend a family gathering, and 88 percent never go to an Easter religious service. Two-thirds indicate that they never attend any other Christian service.

In sum, the Christian influences of these converts center mainly on Christmas involvements with relatives and the exchange of presents, and only 10 percent actually have a tree in their home. Additionally, about a third do occasionally attend Christian services.

Major Jewish Ethnic Involvements

Table 3.14 presents the involvements of these converts in activities in the Jewish community that are not religious in nature. We have included membership in synagogue-related groups, since these groups generally engage in social, cultural, and community service activities without a religious focus.

TABLE 3.14
MAJOR PATTERNS IN CONVERT INVOLVEMENT IN THE JEWISH COMMUNITY

	Frequently		Never	
Jewish Ethnic Practice*	Number	Percent	Number	Percent
Have Jewish art or religious items on display	253	79%	67	21%
Watch Jewish TV or films	207	65%	8	3%
Subscribe to a Jewish newspaper	171	54%	148	46%
Wear Jewish jewelry	135	42%	100	31%
Read Jewishly related literature	125	39%	36	11%
Belong to a Jewish organization	120	38%	200	62%
Participate in ongoing Jewish education	93	29%	228	71%
Belong to a synagogue-related group	89	28%	232	72%
Attend Jewish lectures	61	19%	58	18%
Attend Jewish groups	58	18%	119	37%
Attend Jewish cultural events	49	15%	42	13%
Listen to Jewish music	38	12%	93	29%
Serve as an officer for a Jewish organization	35	11%	242	75%
Belong to a YMHA or Jewish community center	31	10%	285	90%
Teach or organize Jewish activities	27	8%	242	75%

	Number	percent
Importance of Ethnic Activities**		
Live near good public school	240	76%
Support for Israel	225	71%
Visit to Israel	220	70%
Have a substantial number of Jewish neighbors	198	63%
Aliyah to Israel for others	129	43%
Live near Jewish day school	108	34%
Aliyah to Israel for self	86	29%
Percent Jewish Neighbors		
None	15	5%
Don't know	40	13%
less than 15%	94	29%
15%–44%	114	36%
45% or more	55	17%

Yearly Amount Given to Jewish Charities

None	28	9%
$50 or less	42	13%
$51–$300	118	37%
$301–$1,000	80	25%
Above $1,000	51	16%

Percent of Yearly Giving to Jewish Charities

None	20	6%
1%–25%	50	15%
26%–49%	43	14%
50%–60%	66	20%
100%	144	45%

*Categories are collapsed to include "often" and "almost always" responses.
**Categories are collapsed to include "somewhat" and "very important" responses.

Here converts' primary involvement appears fairly private—having Jewish art (79 percent), watching Jewish-oriented films on TV (65 percent), and subscribing to a Jewish newspaper (54 percent) as the top three. Active involvement is low—90 percent do not belong to a Jewish community center, 75 percent do not serve as officers or organize Jewish activities, 71 percent do not participate in lectures or other Jewish cultural events, and 62 percent do not belong to any Jewish organization. They do feel that support for Israel is important (71 percent), including visiting Israel (70 percent), but *alliyah* (moving to Israel) is not highly valued. While only 10 percent have visited Israel, 82 percent plan eventually to do so, with two-thirds planning one visit during their lifetime. Two-thirds feel having Jewish neighbors is important, and most do have some Jewish neighbors, although only 17 percent live in neighborhoods with high concentrations of Jews (45 percent or more). Almost all give to Jewish charities (9 percent do not), and almost half (45 percent) give only to Jewish causes.

It seems then that by an absolute standard, convert ethnic involvement is rather low. They do support Israel and Jewish charities, but few are actively involved in the Jewish community either in attending Jewish cultural events or in membership in Jewish organizations. While most have some Jewish neighbors, most do not live in communities with high concentrations of Jews, and they feel it more important to live near a good public school than near a Jewish day school. Their attachment seems primarily to participation in the major religious holidays. What we might term ethnic involvement is much lower. Except for support for Jewish charities, converts engage in private expressions of Jewish culture through objects and film but are not very actively involved in the Jewish community beyond the family level.

We will compare their profiles with Jewish norms in the next chapter but clearly, in any absolute sense, these converts as a group are not especially strong supporters of either Jewish religious practices or of Jewish culture. However, since these converts start as outsiders and the majority are fairly new converts, these patterns may actually reflect a strong commitment if viewed as a beginning involvement. Also, since these converts are fairly young, their current pattern of community involvement may be reduced by family and career obligations typical of young professionals who later in life tend to become more involved. If their community involvement seems somewhat low, what about their role in passing on a Jewish identity to their children?

Major Patterns of Child Socialization

A little more than half (57 percent) of the converts had children at the time we questioned them. Almost half already had at least one child, averaging between three and five years of age, at the time of their conversion. The number of children ranged from one to five with most having two children. Half had a child under one year of age, and half had all their children under six years of age. Therefore, the questions of identity and of actual practice shown in Table 3.15 represent responses for those with children old enough to participate. The remaining questions on parental values that will guide their raising of their children apply to all convert parents; parental goals may not be followed, but it is unlikely that children will be more involved than their parents intend. We asked for information about the practices of their oldest and their youngest child. Since about a quarter had children ten years or older at the time of their conversion, but only 10 percent had their youngest child of that age, the information on the youngest child may more accurately reflect the influence of the convert's Jewish commitment. When there was only one child in the family, that child was classified as the oldest.

Three-fourths of the convert parents indicated that their children accepted a Jewish identity. However, while a quarter indicated their

TABLE 3.15
MAJOR PATTERNS IN CONVERT COMMITMENT TO JEWISH CHILD-REARING FOCUSES

	Youngest		Oldest	
Variable	Number	Percent	Number	Percent
Religious Identity of Children				
None	12	11%	20	12%
Christianity	15	14%	24	14%
Combined Judaism and Christianity	2	2%	1	0%
Judaism	80	73%	122	74%
Attendance by Child at Synagogue*				
Never	22	25%	38	27%
Infrequently	32	36%	47	33%
Occasionally	15	17%	23	16%
Frequently	20	22%	35	24%
Attendance by Child at Jewish Activities (Not Worship)*				
Never	23	27%	37	26%
Infrequently	32	37%	56	39%
Occasionally	6	7%	13	9%
Frequently	25	29%	38	26%
Attendance by Child at Christian Service*				
Never	61	64%	90	61%
Infrequently	24	26%	44	30%
Occasionally	7	7%	5	3%
Frequently	3	3%	9	6%
Plan to Restrict Child's Dating to Jews				
No	93	83%	141	80%
Uncertain	16	14%	28	16%
Yes	3	3%	8	4%
Importance of General Religious Practices for Children**				
Believing in God	167	93%		
Being free to choose own religion	138	79%		

Importance of Jewish Religious
Practices for Children**

Circumcision or dedication	150	84%
A *Bar* or *Bat Mitzvah*	147	84%
A Jewish part-time education	143	81%
A Hebrew name	142	80%
Believing that Jesus was not the Messiah	98	57%
Confirmation	90	52%
A Jewish day school education	72	42%
Not participating in school Christmas or Easter celebration	62	36%

Importance of Christian Practices
for Children**

Having positive beliefs about Jesus' ministry	52	30%
Attending Christian religious services	12	7%
Being baptized	12	7%

Importance of Jewish Ethnic
Involvements for Children**

Having a strong Jewish identity	147	84%
Raising a Jewish family	140	80%
Having a few Jewish friends	131	78%
Visiting Israel	113	65%
Marrying a Jew (or convert)	86	49%
Attending a Jewish summer camp	78	45%
Having mostly Jewish friends	65	37%
Study in Israel	51	30%
Dating only Jews	47	28%
Aliyah to Israel	46	27%

*Highest and lowest categories are collapsed.
**Categories are collapsed to include "somewhat" and "very important" responses.

child (children) *never* participated in Jewish religious or social activities, a quarter indicated frequent participation. In other words, half of the children were involved in a limited manner (with one-third infrequently). While two-thirds of the children never attended a Christian religious service, a substantial one-third had done so, though mostly on an infrequent basis. Undoubtedly of greatest concern to the survival of the Jewish community is the fact that 80 percent of the converts do not plan to restrict their children's dating to Jews, and only 4 percent are sure they will do so. Perhaps in our open freedom-oriented society, dating restrictions are seen as archaic, so let us look at the values these convert parents hold for their children's Jewish identity.

They virtually all (93 percent) want their children to believe in God but are reluctant to restrict their child's freedom to choose their own religion (79 percent). Since they themselves have changed their religion, perhaps such openness to change is understandable. Eighty percent or more feel the Jewish rites of passage—circumcision/dedication, with a Hebrew name and a *bar* or *bat mitzvah*—are important, but only half want their child to participate in Judaism enough to be confirmed. They prefer a part-time Jewish education (81 percent) to a full-time Jewish day school education (42 percent). Two-thirds are concerned about their children not participating in school Christian holiday celebrations, and 57 percent do not want their children to view Jesus as the Messiah. Nor do they generally want to encourage active Christian participation for their children, such as attending Christian worship services (7 percent) or being baptized (7 percent). Actually, though, between a third and a half of their children have participated in Christian services.

We could say that on the religious side of things, converts do seem to be basically oriented toward Judaism for their children. The problem for ensuring the continuation of a Jewish identity to the third generation is seen in the converts' views about their children's involvement in the Jewish community. As we have seen, while converts may support their children's religious identity as a Jew, they believe their children should have the right to choose, and while 84 percent want their children to have a strong Jewish identity and to raise a Jewish family (80 percent), only one-third want their children to have mostly Jewish friends. While two-thirds want their children to visit Israel, only one-third want them to study there, and even fewer (28 percent) to move there. Nor do most want their children to move in largely Jewish circles as they grow up. However, a substantial minority (45 percent) support having their child (children) attend a Jewish summer camp, and one-third want their child (children) to have mostly Jewish friends. Most telling, only a quarter (27 percent) feel it is important for their child to date only Jews, in spite of the fact that half (49 percent) want them to marry a Jew (or a convert to Judaism).

We can certainly predict that if 20 percent to 50 percent of born

Jews are out-marrying, the children of these converts who are not likely to receive a strong in-marriage message, who move in circles of mostly gentile friends, and who date gentiles are also not very likely to in-marry.

There is very little data yet on the offspring of conversionary marriages. Our data can be compared with that gathered by Egon Mayer in 1983. His data along with ours tend to support Jewish community concerns that such children will be lost entirely or marginal at best. As Mayer points out:

> Particularly in mixed marriages, neither parent wants to inject "too much" Jewishness or Christianity into the children's upbringing lest they become confused by their own family circumstances or actually become biased against one of their parents. Often the net effect of such caution is to deny children substantial access to either tradition beyond the occasional celebration of important religious holidays (1985, p. 246).

At the same time as expressing these concerns about the kind of identity conveyed to the children of intermarrieds, Mayer also discusses what he calls the "tenacity of Jewishness." He notes that among intermarrieds, 73 percent of the born Jews retain their Jewish identity, while only 58 percent of the Protestant and 33 percent of the Catholic spouses retain theirs. The gentile spouse also expresses more interest in Judaism (30 percent) than does the Jew for Christianity (15 percent) (1985, p. 156). The children of intermarriages studied by Mayer were three times more likely to identify themselves religiously as Jews than as Christians. In the conversionary marriages of Mayer's study, 84 percent of the children identified themselves as Jews, none as Christians; in Mayer's mixed marriage group, 24 percent of the children considered themselves Jews, 26 percent Christians (1985, p. 253). At the same time, the children's ethnic identity tended to be an amalgam of both parents. Children had a higher Jewish ethnic identity (50 percent) if their fathers were Jewish and if their gentile mother converted to Judaism (1985, p. 254).

Table 3.16 summarizes some of the data on the religious and ethnic-oriented experiences of children of intermarrieds from Mayer's and our studies. The data are similar on those measures we share. Conversionary children clearly have more Jewish and less Christian-oriented religious experiences as children. In Mayer's study, about three-quarters of the children of conversionary marriages, but fewer than one-third of mixed marriages, maintained involvement in Hanukah, a Passover seder, and High Holiday activities. About one-third of the children of mixed marriages received a Christian-oriented experience that they maintained as adults. Both groups observed Christmas and, to a lesser extent, Easter and continued doing so as adults. Both groups expressed very favorable attitudes toward Jews and Jewish causes. Of concern is the fact that although 84 percent of conversionary children identify themselves as Jewish, two-thirds of them marry gentiles; fewer than half want their children to be identified as Jews, and only a quarter would oppose their own child's marriage to a gentile.

In sum, Mayer's study shows and ours suggests that children of mixed marriages generally have little involvement in and contribution to make to Judaism or the Jewish community, although they do have favorable attitudes toward Jews. About three-quarters of the children of conversionary marriages are involved in major Jewish religious observances, and they tend to evidence more communal/ethnic identification and involvement than do children of mixed marriages. Yet even for this group, marriage to a gentile is the rule, and they do not have a strong concern about the Jewish identity and commitment of their own children. Mayer's information is based on a small group of 117 children from only 71 conversionary intermarried families. Whether these experiences prove to be typical remains to be seen.

Certainly both our data and Mayer's suggest that the Jewish community has cause to be concerned about the future contributions of these children. It appears that only a small group of the children of intermarriages will actually be able to add strength directly to the Jewish community, although they do retain a positive regard and concern for Jews. Additionally, Goldstein and Goldscheider (1968) found that intermarrieds tended to have lower fertility rates than the already low rate for Jews as a whole. Twenty-six percent of intermarrieds remain childless compared with 10 percent of born Jewish pairs. Those who do have children produce 1.6 versus 2.2 children for Jews.

SUMMARY OF PARTICIPANTS' FINDINGS

We have covered quite a bit of information in this chapter but now have some answers to four basic questions: (1) What characteristics

TABLE 3.16
SUMMARY OF RELIGIOUS AND ETHNICALLY ORIENTED EXPERIENCES IN THE FORSTER-TABACHNIK AND MAYER STUDIES

Variable	Percent Forster-Tabachnik As Child/Teen Conversionary	Percent Mayer			
		As Child/Teen		As Adult	
		Conversionary	Mixed	Conversionary	Mixed
Religious—Jewish					
Circumcised	84 *	84	24	—	35
Participate in a Seder	85 **	100	37	79	30
Light Hanukah Candles	82 **	92	33	76	—
Bar/Bat Mitzvah	84 *	90	14	—	—
Religious Identity as a Jew	73	84	24	66	18
Attend Yom Kippur Services	81 **	88	20	—	—
Jewish Education	81 (part-time)* 42 (day school)*	85	20	—	—
Observe Sabbath	47 **	50	6	21	4

Fast on Yom Kippur	67 **	44	6	—	—
Member of Synagogue	69 **	—	—	38	3
Attend Jewish Activity	29	—	—	—	—
Attend Synagogue Regularly	22	22	0	—	—
Plan to Restrict Dating	3 *	—	—	—	—
Religious—Christian					
Observe Christmas	74 **	65	95	70	95
Gave Christmas Presents	25 **	59	93	—	53
Attend Church	36	36	64	4	—
Decorate Christmas Tree	10 **	22	81	—	53
Observe Easter	28 **	19	80	19	53
Christian Education	7	0	50	—	—
Baptized	7	0	28	—	—
Confirmed	—	0	20	—	—
Member of Church	—	—	—	0	25

*Importance by parent rather than actual behavior.

**Convert behavior representing parental influences on children's behaviors.

are associated with those drawn to Judaism, (2) What are the levels of convert adherence to Jewish beliefs and behaviors, (3) What are the ethnic beliefs and involvements of converts, and (4) How strong are the plans of converts to raise Jewishly involved and committed children?

Background Characteristics

Converts tend to come from middle-class, well-educated, affluent backgrounds. They are "pushed" toward Judaism by fairly religious parents who had a positive regard for and some involvement with Jews. They have a high regard for religious involvement but experience some dissatisfaction with Christianity. They are "pulled" toward Judaism by positive interactions with Jews and by involvement with a Jewish partner who values a Jewish identity and life-style. Parents and friends support the intermarriage and conversion. Converts are drawn to Judaism both by religious and by family (marital) considerations.

Convert Adherence to Jewish Beliefs and Practices

Conversion brought a major change in religious beliefs and life-style, but converts were aided in these changes. Their support for traditional Jewish religious beliefs is mixed. Monotheism, free will, and the Jewish covenantal relationship with God are highly accepted, but other Jewish religious beliefs are strongly held by only a minority. Ten percent continue to hold major Christian beliefs. They know the requirements for a Passover seder, Yom Kippur, and the Sabbath observances.

Hanukah, Passover, and the High Holidays in that order are the favored practices for these converts. Two-thirds belong to a synagogue, but fewer than one-fourth regularly attend Sabbath services and engage in home ritual. Only 16 percent avoid work on the Sabbath. While they believe continued study is important, most are not regularly involved in Jewish education.

The Christian practices retained by these converts mainly involve Christmas celebrations with their relatives and the exchange of presents; only 10 percent have a Christmas tree in their own home. However, about one-third do occasionally attend Christian services.

Jewish Ethnic Beliefs and Involvements

Converts do generally support Jewish ethnic issues, with the important exception of not being concerned whether their children marry a Jew or not. They know little of Jewish history except the Holocaust and report being mostly ignorant about Jewish community resources. Their own ethnic involvement is fairly private—having Jewish art objects, watching Jewish-oriented media programs, and subscribing to a Jewish newspaper. They are not very active in Jewish community affairs, although they do give to Jewish causes. While two-thirds feel it is important to live in a Jewish neighborhood, only 17 percent actually do.

Plans for Child Socialization

While three-quarters of these converts' children reportedly accept a Jewish identity, only one-quarter are actively involved in Judaism. Converts believe that their children should choose their own religion, want them to have mixed social groups with mostly gentile friends, and are not very concerned about whether or not their children marry Jews.

Additional Considerations

Analysis of major subgroups in our data has led us to several additional understandings that we will present here in summary form only. First, the most and the least religiously serious converts differ little in beliefs but much in self-reported Jewish knowledge and in practice and ethnic involvements. This finding lends some support for the validity of the Jewish focus on behaviors over beliefs, since in our data converts' beliefs tend to be similar even when their practice differs substantially. They do not differ in their child socialization patterns, being concerned most with permitting their children religious choice and freedom in relationships with gentiles while at the same time wishing for a Jewish identity by their children.

Second, male and female converts do not differ significantly.

Third, Reform and Conservative converts are mostly similar, but where they do differ, as to be expected, Conservative converts tend to be more traditional in practices while Reform converts tend a bit more to hold on to Christian practices.

Fourth, we compared those converts who had no Jewish partner attachment for their conversion (48, or 15 percent) with those who did (262, or 85 percent). If the marital motive produces bogus outcomes, our data do not indicate it; the two groups were essentially the same in observance of specific rituals; however, nonattached converts observed more rituals overall.

Fifth, "dropouts" from the Introduction to Judaism course had already developed ethnic involvements and basic Jewish knowledge. It may be that they are accepted and knowledgeable enough to make further study and conversion unnecessary as far as they are concerned. Nonconverts tend to be males with less support for conversion, more Christian beliefs, and less concern about a Jewish identity for themselves or their children.

Finally, for those students who persist, the introductory course seems to help in the areas of Jewish knowledge and practice skills, but participants show a lack of information about Jewish community resources and do not change their child-rearing orientations.

From an absolute standard, only about a quarter of these converts seem to be especially strong adherents to Judaism and contributors to the Jewish community. However, in the next chapter we will turn our attention to comparing the converts' situations with that of their partners and of born Jews.

4

Convert Comparisons with Partners and Other Born Jews

IN THE LAST chapter we looked in detail at information about converts to Judaism. Our frame of reference for their behaviors was an absolute standard; that is, how far were they from total, traditional practice. While purists may prefer an absolute standard, in reality converts enter a community, and they are influenced by and gauge their behaviors by the Jewish community they join. In order to judge converts by that social reality we need to look at the practices of their Jewish partners who provide major influences and then of born Jews in the community in which these converts interact.

PATTERNS IN PARTNER BACKGROUND CHARACTERISTICS

Who are the Jewish partners? Our information comes from two sources—Jewish partners attending the conversion classes with gentile students (110, 45 percent) and partners of previous students who agreed to help with the mail-in questionnaire (136, 55 percent). Since the partner responses showed little significant differences between these two groups, we have combined their information for this discussion. Jewish partners are encouraged to attend the Introduction to Judaism course. Not only does their attendance encourage discussion and sharing between the partners about the issues raised, but partners acquire new and renewed information about Judaism for themselves. Most partners do participate.

Since our objective is to compare the convert and partner data, we have grouped the partner measures as we did for converts. In the case of Jewish partners' backgrounds, PUSH factors are those that might "push" them toward interaction with gentiles, assimilation (or at least acculturation), and intermarriage. PULL factors are those that attract them to gentile partners. First we will take a look at partner patterns, then we will compare partner backgrounds with those of born Jews to see how Jews who marry gentiles differ from those who in-marry.

Two-thirds of the 246 partners are males from well-educated families (one-third of their fathers had postgraudate and two-thirds had a college education; 40 percent of their mothers were college educated). Half of the partners have postgraduate education, 40 percent are in professional jobs, and two-thirds earn $75,000 a year or more.

Table 4.1 shows PUSH background factors for partners that are comparable to convert patterns shown in Table 3.3. We'll look first at some comparisons of parental PUSH influences, then at individual background factors.

Parental PUSH Influences

In comparing Jewish partner and convert parental influence we find that partners reported better relationships with their parents than did converts. Eighty-one percent reported good relationships with their fathers (62 percent for converts) and 91 percent with their mothers (73 percent for converts). Both partners and converts reported somewhat better relationships with their mothers than with their fathers.

While partners' parents generally had a high percentage of Jewish friends, the range was as low as 5 percent. Perhaps reflecting their respective majority-minority status, Jewish parents were more likely to have gentile friends than gentile parents were Jewish ones: only 2 percent of the Jewish parents had no gentile friends while more than a quarter of the gentile parents lacked Jewish friends. The partners also tended to have gentile friends in adolescence (only 8 percent did not compared with 60 percent of converts without Jewish friends), while the converts tended to gain their Jewish friends after leaving home.

Finally, Jewish parents were not overly positive about gentiles. Eighty percent of partner parents had positive attitudes toward Jewish people, about a quarter had positive views toward gentiles. Overall, this was a somewhat less favorable view of the other group by Jewish than by gentile parents (a quarter of Jewish parents had

TABLE 4.1
PATTERNS IN JEWISH PARTNERS' BACKGROUND
PUSH FACTORS

Variable	Number	Percent
Sex		
Female	86	32%
Male	160	68%
Adolescent Relationship to Father*		
Strained	43	19%
Basically Good	179	81%
Adolescent Relationship to Mother*		
Strained	22	9%
Basically Good	223	91%
Percent of Father's Friends as Jews		
Range		5–100%
Average		68.35%
Most Common		90%
Percent of Mother's Friends as Jews		
Range		5–100%
Average		73.21%
Most common		90%
Father's View of Gentiles*		
Negative	51	24%
Mixed	106	50%
Positive	56	26%
Mother's View of Gentiles*		
Negative	50	22%
Mixed	114	51%
Positive	59	27%
Father's Gentile Friends*		
None	3	1%
Some	172	74%
Many	58	25%
Mother's Gentile Friends*		
None	5	3%
Some	124	66%
Many	59	31%

Own Gentile Friends as Adolescent*

None	21	9%
Some	102	43%
Many	113	48%

Own Political Views*

Basically Conservative	43	17%
Moderate	88	36%
Basically Liberal	115	47%

Personal Religious Participation

None	11	5%
Little	134	58%
Regular	88	37%

Years of Formal Religious Instruction
Average: 7 ½ Years
Most Frequent: 10 Years

Jewish Religious Group Identified With

None	7	3%
Reform	142	57%
Conservative	68	27%
Other	31	13%

Bar or Bat Mitzvah

No	54	23%
Yes	186	77%

Confirmed

No	123	53%
Yes	108	47%

Dissatisfaction with Judaism*

Dissatisfied	36	15%
Neutral	70	29%
Satisfied	134	56%

Certainty of God's Existence*

Don't Believe God Exists	18	8%
Uncertain Whether God Exists	144	61%
Certain God Exists	76	31%

Adolescent View about Jesus

Doubt His Existence	73	31%
A Great Teacher	143	61%
Best of Humans	12	5%
Called by God	7	3%
Divine	0	0%

Adult View about Jesus

Doubt His Existence	48	20%
A Great Teacher	166	69%
Best of Humans	18	8%
Called by God	7	3%
Divine	0	0%

Father's Involvement in Jewish Community*

None	44	18%
Little	105	42%
Much	102	40%

Mother's Involvement in Jewish Community*

None	37	15%
Little	93	38%
Much	114	47%

*Categories are collapsed with the negative and positive categories containing both "somewhat" and "strongly so" responses.

negative views of gentiles, while only about 15 percent of the gentile parents disliked Jews).

Individual PUSH Influences

These partners and converts share political orientations with a leaning toward liberal. The majority (57 percent) of partners identified with Reform Judaism. A third came from religiously active homes, a third were from religiously inactive homes, two-thirds had some kind of part-time Jewish education averaging seven and a half years, but only one third were themselves regularly religiously active (compared with 54 percent for their partners). Three Jewish partners' mothers and one father were reported as being Christians, and 5 percent reported mothers who changed religions. Partner participation in important religious rites of adolescence was a bit less than converts for confirmation (47 percent of partners versus 65 percent of converts), but three-quarters had a *bar* or *bat mitzvah*. (The fact that 88 percent of Christians were baptized is not comparable, since Christian baptism often is done on infants.) As might be expected, Jewish partners were more satisfied with their religion (56 percent) than was true for the converts (14 percent). Jewish partners were somewhat less sure about God's existence and less positive about Jesus: as adolescents more Jews doubted even the existence of Jesus (31 percent versus 12 percent for the gentiles) and tended to see him as a great teacher (69 percent versus 57 percent).

About 40 percent of partner parents were actively involved in the Jewish community.

In sum, partners and their Jewishly oriented parents tended to be drawn to gentiles as friends but tended to retain a high satisfaction with their own religious and ethnic identity. Though they were somewhat less religiously active than were the converts, partners were involved in Jewish community affairs. For these partners PUSH factors seem only to indicate contact opportunity with gentiles but not a real push out of the Jewish community.

What about factors that would tend to "pull" the Jewish partner toward serious involvement with a gentile? Table 4.2 summarizes major partner patterns for those pulls; this information is to be compared with the convert information in Tables 3.4 and 3.5. Here we will examine the attraction (PULLs) that serious contact with a gentile and her family evidenced.

Parental PULL Influences

As already indicated, most Jewish partners had fairly active involvements with gentile friends while still adolescents. This friendly contact eventually led to a serious involvement with a gentile and her family. It seems to be the personal appeal of an individual gentile rather than a family attraction that draws the Jewish partner into a permanent relationship. Three-quarters of the Jews felt that their own family relationships were as good as or even better than their gentile partner's family relationships (only 54 percent of the gentiles thought their family relationships were better than their partner's), and they reported getting negative parental reactions about their serious involvement with a gentile (50 percent of their fathers disapproved, 56 percent of their mothers disapproved). However, they did get support from their Jewish and gentile friends for the potential intermarriage (82 percent and 84 percent respectively approved).

Only about a quarter of the partners indicated that their gentile partners' parents disapproved of the intermarriage. The Jews tended to see the gentile partner and her parents as not very religiously active, attributing no meaningful religious involvement to 50 percent of the partners, 42 percent of their fathers, and 28 percent of

TABLE 4.2
PATTERNS IN JEWISH PARTNERS' BACKGROUND
PULL FACTORS

Variable*	Number	Percent
Gentile Friends as Adolescent		
None	21	9%
Some	102	43%
Many	113	48%
Gentile Partner's Family Relationships Compared with Own		
Not as Close	117	48%
Same	71	29%
Closer	54	23%
Own Father's Reaction to Intermarriage		
Disapproval	90	50%
Neutral	26	14%
Approval	64	36%
Own Mother's Reaction to Intermarriage		
Disapproval	113	56%
Neutral	26	10%
Approval	69	34%
Own Friends' Reaction to Intermarriage		
Disapproval	20	9%
Neutral	22	9%
Approval	191	82%
Partner's Father's Reaction to Intermarriage		
Disapproval	50	27%
Neutral	41	22%
Approval	95	61%
Partner's Mother's Reaction to Intermarriage		
Disapproval	59	28%
Neutral	36	17%
Approval	115	55%
Partner's Friends' Reaction to Intermarriage		
Disapproval	24	12%
Neutral	29	14%
Approval	155	74%

Partner's Religious Activity
None	120	50%
Some	99	42%
Regular	19	8%

Partner's Father's Religious Activity
None	84	42%
Some	65	33%
Regular	49	25%

Partner's Mother's Religious Activity
None	60	28%
Some	87	40%
Regular	70	32%

Reaction to Christian Partner's Religious Services
Basically Dislike	95	59%
Neutral	41	26%
Basically Like	24	15%

Desire to Learn about Christian Partner's Religion
None	34	14%
Neutral	59	25%
Some	129	54%
Much	16	7%

Interest in Converting to Christianity
None	226	94%
Some	15	6%

Feelings about Partner Not Being a Jew
Dislike	101	43%
Neutral	47	20%
Mixed	81	35%
Like	5	2%

Siblings Intermarriage
No	150	66%
Yes	78	34%

Siblings Marriage to Convert
No	205	91%
Yes	21	9%

Own Father's View of Partner's Conversion
Disapproval	7	4%
Neutral	12	7%
Approval	155	89%

Own Mother's View of Partner's Conversion		
Disapproval	11	5%
Neutral	7	4%
Approval	186	91%
Attempt to Draw Gentile Partner to Judaism		
None	104	42%
Some	108	44%
Much	36	14%
Personal Importance for Partner to Convert		
Don't Want	1	0%
Neutral	56	24%
Want	179	76%

*Categories are collapsed with the negative and positive categories containing both "somewhat" and "strongly so" responses.

their mothers, and regular activity to only 8 percent of the gentile partners, 25 percent of their fathers, and 32 percent of their mothers. Converts, however, indicate a much higher level of activity for their parents and themselves (50 percent to 60 percent reported active). Partners' perceptions of a weak religious commitment from the gentile side may have helped them feel that a request for conversion would not bring a serious conflict. A third of the partners already had siblings who had intermarried, but only 9 percent to converts, which means that they already knew the consequences of a mixed marriage to their family. The pull from the gentile family side seems rather weak on the Jewish partners, and is clearly weaker than the Jewish family's attractiveness to the gentile partner.

Individual PULL Influences

Most partners were not drawn to their gentile partners' religion: 59 percent disliked Christian services, one-third weren't much interested in learning about Christianity, and only a handful (6 percent) had ever considered converting themselves. On the other hand, they weren't too happy about their partner not being Jewish (only 2 percent thought it was fine), and their own parents were very supportive of the gentile converting (90 percent approved). They themselves tended to want their partner to convert (70 percent) and even put some effort into persuading them to do so (58 percent).

Most of these Jewish partners indicated that their own commitment to Judaism and the Jewish people had increased as adults. About three-quarters wanted to increase their observance, while 48 percent indicated their Jewish practice had increased as adults. Two-thirds liked Jewish traditions, and over half (53 percent) felt a stronger attachment to the Jewish people as adults than as children, with two-thirds involved in learning more about their religion as adults. All of this supports the picture given us previously by the converts who depicted their Jewish partners as fairly seriously committed to being a Jew.

We might pause here to consider the issue of the cause(s) of intermarriage by Jews. What are the most important influences? Most existing information about causes of Jewish out-marriage is speculative and inferential rather than by report of the out-marrieds themselves. Figure 4.1 summarizes the various reasons for out-marriage by Jews that have been proposed.

What do our data show? Our data seem to support a more sociological than psychological explanation for these Jewish males (the majority of our partners). The Jewish partners had good relationships with their parents, a majority of Jewish friends, but a substantial number of gentile friends even in adolescence, a basic Jewish education, and satisfaction with Judaism. While it is true we don't have direct measures for all of the psychological dimensions, we have enough to conclude that psychological factors are an unlikely reason, at least for this group. They do have parents with gentile friends, go to public schools (and later to colleges) with gentiles, find themselves accepted by and even attractive to gentiles, and sense little resistance to their involvement. All of this suggests that the societal-level explanations are more weighty. Nor do they seem to be using intermarriage as a step toward leaving the Jewish fold. In fact, their commitment to a Jewish identity is strong enough to enable them to encourage and support conversion by their gentile partner. And their Jewish education seems at least as good as, if not better than, the average in-marrying Jew.

In short, the strongest PULL factor for these Jewish partners seemed to be attraction to a gentile on personal grounds. They even preferred that their partner take on Judaism rather than become involved in Christianity themselves, because they wanted to retain their Jewish connection and identity, and they felt uncomfortable affirming Christian beliefs. They tended to actively encourage conversion. This last finding is to be expected from our group, since we

FIGURE 4.1
SUMMARY OF REASONS PROPOSED TO EXPLAIN
JEWISH INTERMARRIAGE

Social—Societal Level

—Urbanization, modernism, secularization
—Decreasing importance of religion
—Decreased opposition by gentiles (Vatican II)
—Values of individualism, personalism, and privatism in family life
—Romantic love as marriage ideal
—American ideal of blonde, blue-eyed WASP
—Return of the valuation of ethnicity
—Jewish group reputation (good provider, strong families)
—Shortage of eligible Jewish partners

Social—Group Level

—Egalitarianism, tolerance, brotherhood values
—Dispersion of the Jewish community
—Decreased Jewish density and cohesiveness
—Increased gentile contact
—Strong marriage ethic
—Jewish prince (princess) image of Jew about other Jews
—Increase in interdating
—Children raised less to carry tradition—permissive, individualistic
—Decreased resistance to intermarriage

Social-Psychological—Individual Interpersonal Level

—Nativity
—Lack of Jewish education
—Marginality to the Jewish community
—Education, occupation, housing in mixed settings
—Life-style, recreation, activities same as dominant (acculturation)
—Few kin ties
—Age (younger for females, older for males)
—Remarriage

Psychological—Personal

—Youngest or only child—Ambition to succeed
—Status seeking
—Existential insecurity/group hatred
—Identification with the powerful
—Escape from burden of Jewishness
—Escape from anti-Semitism

—Excessive attachment to same sex parent
—Excessively overprotective parent(s)
—Repressive sexual training
—Troubled relation with parents as adolescent
—Sexual taboo violation
—Divorce of parents

are studying those couples who had sought formal means of pursuing Judaism together; however, we must remember that this group represents only about one-third of Jewish-gentile intermarriages.

COMPARISONS AMONG GROUPS

In order to understand how our information about Jewish partners fits the larger context, we now turn our attention to a comparison among our three groups—in-married born Jews, intermarried Jewish partners, and converts. Having been selected for our study by their rabbis, our in-married born Jews represent the religiously involved community. The Jewish partners' group is composed of partners attending the Introduction to Judaism course and partners of former students who mailed in their questionnaires. In order to facilitate the reader's focusing on the major comparisons, the more detailed tables are located in the Appendix. Readers who wish to pursue those details are invited to turn to the appropriate Appendix tables. Here we will identify the major trends and differences.

In our comparisons we are not differentiating Reform from Conservative Jews or males from females. As we have indicated, insofar as there are differences between Conservative and Reform Jews, Reform Jews evidence somewhat lower scores on Jewish beliefs, knowledge, practices, and child socialization and more Christian beliefs and practices, with greater differences found on these variables between Reform and Conservative males than females. Generally, Jewish males show slightly higher religious practice and knowledge scores but lower acceptance of Jewish beliefs than females.

We are also putting the partner and partner course information together in our comparisons. Partners of converts tended to show slightly higher levels of practice than did partner course participants; otherwise they were similar. Since the student groups contained both persons who would eventually convert and those who would not do so, we have not included their data. Finally, respondents who finished the course and decided not to convert are not included in most of our comparisons because we are more interested in the behavior of converts. As might be expected, nonconverts showed significantly lower scores than the converts on most of our measures for Jewish beliefs, practices, and child socialization and higher scores on our measures of Christian beliefs and practices. They tended to have had a less positive experience with Jews than converts and a stronger Christian background. Keeping these distinctions in mind, we will proceed with a simplified analysis, just comparing the three major categories—religiously involved in-married Jews, partners, and converts.

Background PUSH Variables

Our convert group tended to be females (80 percent versus 20 percent); partners, males (73 percent versus 27 percent); and born Jews, about equally males and females (46 percent males, 54 percent females). (See Table 4.3, Appendix.) Comparing in-married born Jews to intermarried Jewish partners, partners tended to come from families who were *more* positive about and involved with gentiles than did in-married Jews.

A common belief in the Jewish community is that intermarrying Jews lack a Jewish education. However, our data indicate that partners tended to have had significantly more Jewish religious instruction than in-married Jews. Our in-married, religiously committed Jews had an average two and a half years of formal religious instruction while the partners of converts averaged seven and two-thirds years. Partners also showed significantly higher childhood involvements in Jewish practices, knowledge of the blessings, and ethnic involvements than in-marrieds but also a higher exposure to Christian practices. This higher exposure to Jewish education and involvements runs counter to conventional wisdom that intermarrying Jews lack such a base. Perhaps the conventional wisdom holds for the two-thirds of intermarriages where the gentile does not convert, but it is not true for our conversionary partners.

These facts again highlight why these partners are taking advantage of an opportunity to have their gentile partners at least learn about, if not actually convert to, Judaism. They have a fairly strong involvement with Judaism, though a tolerance for Christians and their practices, and they prefer similar behaviors from their partners.

Converts differ from both in-married Jews and their Jewish partners similarly. They have had less positive relationships with their parents, more religiously involved parents, and more religious education, but they also evidence more dissatisfaction with their own religion and questioning about God. They continue to hold more positive views about Jesus.

Background PULL Variables

On the major PULL variables, in-married Jews and intermarried Jewish partners are generally similar in their attraction to Judaism, with the exception that partners are more positive toward converts, though they are less positive toward their partners' gentile families than in-married Jews are toward their Jewish in-laws. (See Table 4.4, Appendix.) While converts view their Jewish partners' family relationships as better than their own, they are less comfortable with their Jewish in-laws than are born Jews, though they see those Jewish in-laws more frequently than their own family. These findings support other data that indicate strong positive family interactions and attractions among Jews (see Chapter 1). What about the quality of the marital interaction? Do intermarrieds have more conflicts than in-marrieds? To the contrary, in-married Jews report more disagreements with each other over religious matters than do partners and converts. Perhaps these out-marrying partners have stronger compatibilities that hold them together in spite of religious differences, or they may have been forced to resolve those differences before proceeding with their relationships.

Converts are less positive about their contributions to Judaism than are their partners and born Jews, and they are more aware of difficulties in converting. While converts do want to be Jews, they feel somewhat less personal importance in being identified as a Jew than either partners or in-marrieds.

Belief Variables

As we've previously indicated, Christians tend to emphasize beliefs; Jews emphasize practice. It is therefore important to consider the extent to which Christian converts' acceptance of Jewish religious and ethnic beliefs is similar to that of born Jews. We shall see that there are important differences in beliefs held by converts and in-married Jews, though less difference in beliefs between converts and their Jewish partners.

First, in the general religious beliefs category, the ranking of beliefs is quite similar for all three groups. (See Table 4.5, Appendix.) Converts are more likely to view prayer as important than are either set of born Jews; converts and partners have more of a sense of the Divine presence in life than in-marrieds; in marrieds talk about religion more than partners or converts. Otherwise they are similar in their belief about God and the place of religion in their lives. The top three and bottom two ranked Jewish beliefs are shared by the three groups—top three: humans have free will, Judaism is more personally true, and there is only one God; bottom two: moral non-Jews will be saved, and God will send the Messiah. Otherwise there is considerable disagreement, especially between in-married Jews and converts. (Converts and partners tend to be similar in how strongly each belief is held.) Partners and converts are more concerned about beliefs than a moral life; converts have stronger beliefs in the convenantal relationship between God and Jews, the Bible as God's revealed word, the salvation of moral non-Jews, and the coming of the promised messiah. While rabbinic Judaism stresses the salvation of all non-Jews who follow the Noahide laws of basic morality, this belief is not shared by these religious Jews. It is not surprising that converts believe moral behavior to be sufficient since they are, by joining Judaism, rejecting the need for salvation through faith in Jesus.

As might be expected, converts hold more Christian beliefs than either set of Jews, although they are equally skeptical about the resurrection. Converts are slightly less likely than either group to believe that Jesus actually broke with Judaism, though all three groups rate this belief strongest. That may explain why they can feel positive about Jesus while still converting to Judaism. They view Jesus as a Jew and as their connector to Judaism. Christians who convert are not likely to see Jesus as do Jews in light of two thousand years of persecution in his name and are more likely to know him from the New Testament accounts that depict him as a persecuted Jew who tried to bring God's message to people. Converts are more likely to believe in his special role.

In the area of ethnic beliefs there is almost a reversal, with converts supporting concerns about the survival of Jews and Judaism that are not the highest concern for Jews. Converts seem most concerned with items that directly affect them—anti-Semitism,

feeling comfortable among Jews—but less concerned about community survival issues—voting for pro-Israel political candidates, supporting Israel, and having Jewish children marry Jews.

A further question about the perception of Jewish beliefs is
possible using the student data. We asked students to estimate what
they felt most Jews would answer to the beliefs questions as well as
to indicate their own beliefs. The extent and accuracy of potential
converts' awareness of Jewish beliefs represents something of the
standard to which they believe they will be held. Readers comparing
Appendix Tables 4.5 and 4.6 will note some differences between
convert beliefs and student beliefs. Generally speaking, the students
have scores somewhat higher than converts on all measures. While
that difference makes sense for the Christian beliefs, since the
student group includes those who decide not to convert in favor of
retaining their Christian identity, the higher scores for Jewish
religious and ethnic beliefs among the students are harder to
explain. It is true, though, that even the converts tended to have
stronger beliefs in all these categories, except the ethnic one, than
did born Jews (including their partners).

Students' views about Jewish beliefs do not significantly change
as a result of the introduction course. While Jews stress practice
over belief, since potential converts tend to be Christians who give
more primacy to beliefs, perhaps more attention needs to be given
to belief issues for potential converts. The greatest belief discrepan-
cies are in converts holding more Christian beliefs and lower ethnic
beliefs than born Jews. Yet converts may misperceive Jewish beliefs,
as we shall see.

We identified significant differences in each of the belief categories between the students' perception of Jewish beliefs, the reported
beliefs of their partners, and their own beliefs. We previously
learned that, generally speaking, partners' beliefs parallel both in-
married born Jews' and converts' beliefs, tending to fall midway
between them. Students tend to significantly underestimate the
general religious, Jewish religious, and ethnic beliefs of religiously
involved Jews. They are fairly accurate in their perception of the
minimal level of Christian beliefs held by Jews, but retain their own
more positive Christian beliefs.

Students believe themselves to be stronger adherents than Jews
to virtually all the beliefs. That misperception may inhibit their
community involvement, which is a less structured situation for
them than the practice of religious rituals. Thinking that Jews

aren't much concerned about ethnic issues and that they themselves are concerned more than most Jews puts potential and actual converts somewhat out of step with at least the religiously involved Jewish community, which strongly supports ethnic issues while being less concerned with religious beliefs. Also, while students recognize the importance to Jews of in-marriage, they retain a significantly lower concern about the matter.

Knowledge Variables

The ranking on the self-reported knowledge perception questions is fairly similar between the three groups. (See Table 4.7, Appendix.) Partners believe themselves less knowledgeable than in-married Jews while converts report more knowledge than either group. It should be remembered that these are self-evaluation questions rather than the results of objective tests. It is possible that Jews have a higher standard for what they consider good knowledge of Judaism because of their exposure to the breadth and depth of Jewish scholarship. On the other hand, it may be that converts, by studying purposefully as adults, indeed know more about Judaism than born Jews. Support for the first explanation, differences in standards, may be gotten from the fact that the converts scored higher than their partners on these items. Not only did the partners have a fairly good level of Jewish education, as we've already seen, but also most of them attended the same classes as the converts yet still rated their knowledge lower. By and large converts did not expend much studying time during or after this introductory course, so it is likely that they are misjudging the state of their knowledge. Some converts, no doubt, do go on to greater knowledge, but that is true of no more than a quarter of this group, as we've previously discussed. Since partners tend to rate themselves as less knowledgeable than in-married Jews even though they had more religious instruction and attended the classes, it may be that the introduction classes served to remind them of how little they knew when exposed to Jewish scholarship represented by the rabbis who taught the courses and by the course readings. Or it may be that they indeed lack knowledge as some commentators on intermarriage surmise. Still, it should be noted that all three groups tended to feel that they had fairly adequate knowledge about Jewish religious requirements.

In awareness of community resources, in-married Jews reported significantly better knowledge than either partners or converts. Since converts are likely to refer to their partners for information they need about resources, it is distressing to see that their partners know little more than they do.

Religious Practices

To what extent do the three grups differ in their religious practices? This is one critical concern in the debates about the role of converts that our previous chapter left unaddressed. Our data show that while there is fairly good agreement between the groups on the rank order of how frequently they engage in the various practices, both partners and converts tend to engage in less Jewish religious practice than religiously involved in-marrieds. (See Table 4.8, Appendix.) Some, but not all, of this difference comes from the fact that the out-marrieds tend to be Reform Jews while our in-married group is somewhat more Conservative. Generally, converts show even lower Jewish practices than their partners, especially for the more popular practices. Converts are more likely than their partners to have a menorah, observe Purim, refrain from Sabbath work, engage in study and prayer, eat kosher outside the home, and say the morning prayers. Unfortunately, our data do not support the observation that converts as a group are better at Jewish religious practices compared with our religious in-married Jews. (As we'll discuss shortly, they may be better when compared with the general Jewish community.) It may also be the case that a minority of converts are more committed and therefore more visible to rabbis. It is also true that our in-married born Jewish sample is somewhat older and thereby more traditional in their practice. Converts may look better when compared with born Jews of similar (younger) ages. In our study we can gauge this probability by comparing the converts with their partners who are similar in age. While there are not as many differences, out of this list of thirty-two practices converts match their partners on fourteen practices, exceed their partners on six practices, and fall short of their partners on twelve practices. This picture would not permit us to say that these converts as a group are "better Jews" than religiously oriented Jews as far as religious practices are concerned. Compared with their partners, these converts are more concerned about continuing to study Judaism, learning the prayers, and living near a synagogue. Whether there are resources to meet these concerns and, if met, whether convert practice would improve, we can only speculate. These responses do seem to indicate a need for accessible continuing education programs for converts. It should be noted that these converts completed their introductory studies before the addition of a basic Hebrew prayers program begun in 1988.

Both these partners and these converts engage in significantly more Christian practices than do in-married Jews, especially relating to Christmas presents and family gatherings. (See Table 4.9, Appendix.) This does not necessarily represent a serious threat to their own Jewish identity but may be a distraction for their children's identity.

Ethnic Involvements

Since the converts' contact with Christian practices is more ethnically (family) than religiously centered, we need to consider the extent of their ongoing involvements in the Jewish community as a potentially counterbalancing force. The top and bottom ranked involvements tend to be similar for all three groups. At the top, all three groups have Jewish art, watch Jewish-oriented TV programs or films, and subscribe to a Jewish newspaper or magazine; at the bottom, they tend not to belong to a Jewish community center or teach or organize Jewish classes or activities. (See Table 4.10, Appendix.) It is the Jewish partners in this case who tend to be the least involved of all three groups. Partners fall significantly behind in-married Jews on thirteen of the fifteen measures while converts fall short on only five measures; and on six measures converts exceed their partners. On balance, then, it seems that converts bring more positive Jewish ethnic involvements to their home life than a look just at their Christmas inputs would indicate, and they may indeed be helping to preserve a Jewish orientation to the household on an ongoing basis. However, they are less concerned about traditional ethnic involvements (Israel, living near Jews, and being near Jewish education) than are in-married Jews.

Children Socialization Plans

Our final major area of concern is the comparisons between the groups on their desire to involve their children Jewishly. Our data indicate that the ranking of concerns is similar between the groups; where there are differences, there is better rank agreement between partners and converts than either of those groups with in-married Jews. (See Table 4.11, Appendix.) However, the degree of concern about their children's Jewish identity and involvement is clearly different; partners and converts fall below born-Jews on the child Jewish involvement measures and above them on child Christian involvement and general choice measures. Partners and converts tend to agree more about the importance of Jewish religious practices for their children than about their ethnic involvements. In the latter case converts fall significantly below their partners in concern about their children's Jewish ethnic involvements. The largest areas of differences concern their children's friendship, dating, and marriage of Jews. We've already discussed this issue in Chapter 3.

COMPARISON OF OUR DATA WITH OTHER STUDIES

Practice Comparisons

Thus far, our comparison of converts with partners and with religiously involved, in-married born Jews would indicate that, as a group, converts are somewhat less involved or committed than Jews. But before we can draw our final conclusions about the contributions and fit of converts to the Jewish community as a whole, we need to know to what extent our born Jewish participants' behaviors are typical. For this we need to look at data from other studies that have incorporated a cross-section of born Jews, not just the religiously committed segment our data reflects. To anticipate our findings, converts' behaviors look much better when compared with Jewish community standards as a whole. The actual extent to which members of the Jewish community personally adhere to the practices advocated by the rabbis has only recently begun to be addressed. What do the data show?

As reported in a study of Jewish identity by Herman, the majority of U.S. Jews see Jews as both a religious group and a people (1977, p. 71), but their own attachment to Judaism as a religion is weak. For example, a Boston study reported by Sklare indicated that Jews attended religious services much less frequently than did the general U.S. population (1971, p. 118). The study found the following comparisons:

	Jews	Gentiles
Attended services more than once a month	17%	65%
Attend services monthly or so	21%	11%
Attend for main holiday only	39%	6%
Attend infrequently or never	23%	18%

Sklare indicated that, in general, Jews wanted their religion to:

1. Be defined in modern terms;
2. Require no social isolation or unique life-style;
3. Fit in with the holiday patterns of the dominant culture;
4. Be centered on child activities, and
5. Be performed annually or infrequently (1971, p. 114).

Generally, Jews wanted a Jewish education only to prepare their children for *bar/bat mitzvah* and confirmation. One study showed this trend by finding that 69.8 percent of eight- to twelve-year-old Jewish children were receiving instruction, but only 15.8 percent of thirteen- to seventeen-year-olds remained in Jewish-oriented programs. Jewish parents prefer a secular education for their children (only 13.4 percent were attending Hebrew day schools) with supplemental Jewish instruction either on Sundays (42.2 percent) or in an afternoon Hebrew school program (44.4 percent) involving a few hours a week only (Sklare, 1971, p. 173).

At the same time, even secular Jews maintain a high level of communal involvement. One study showed that 96 percent of Jews had only Jewish relatives, 77 percent had all their closest friends as Jews, 60 percent belonged to Jewish community organizations, virtually all of them gave to Jewish charities, and 90 percent felt a strong attachment to Israel (Waxman, 1983, p. 139). When asked, however, third generation Jews define themselves as a religious group in spite of their stronger ethnic-oriented practice (Friedman, 1986, pp. 34–37; Waxman, 1983, p. 81). Clearly, though, American Jews are increasingly secularized and interface during much of their educational and occupational life with the gentile world.

For comparing available data on born Jews and intermarrieds, Table 4.12 summarizes the findings of several recent major studies of Jews, including ours. As one can see, not every study provides comparable information. This is a common problem in social science research, but should not deter one from apprehending the general trends. We have chosen to compare the most frequently and consistently measured items.

Most studies provide information about observance of major Jewish religious holidays—Hanukah, Passover, Rosh Hashanah, and Yom Kippur. There is a high rate of observance of these holidays by religiously affiliated Jews and by converts (80 percent to 90 percent observe them), with substantially lower rates of observances by

TABLE 4.12
COMPARISON OF THE FORSTER-TABACHNIK DATA WITH OTHER STUDIES OF BORN JEWS AND INTERMARRIEDS

Variable*	General Communal Study Averages	Forster-Tabachnik Data				Mayer Data	
		Born Jews	Partners	Converts	Mixed	Converts	Mixed
Jewish Religious Practices							
Participate in a Passover seder	89%	96%	87%	93%	79%	95%	37%
Attend Yom Kippur services	86	93	81	87	48	88	20
Light Hanukah candles	84	90	94	86	63	92	33
Attend Rosh Hashanah services	84	91	80	82	46	88	21
Belong to a synagogue	49	99	64	69	29	87	NA
Attend Sabbath services	42	30	26	74	33	67	6
Fast on Yom Kippur	39	65	65	60	27	NA	NA
Light Sabbath candles	35	40	35	63	25	NA	NA
Keep kosher at home	24	21	12	14	11	NA	NA
Christian Religious Practices							
Attend a Christmas family gathering	13	13	56	58	95	65	95
Attend Easter family gatherings	NA	3	32	20	62	19	80
Jewish Ethnic Practices							
Subscribe to a Jewish newspaper	82	65	38	54	16	80	NA
Half or more friends as Jews	81	91	74	35	27	NA	NA
Important to support Israel	78	93	84	85	34	NA	NA
Give to Jewish charities	67	91	91	91	79	81	NA
Belong to a Jewish organization	37	60	27	38	9	67	NA
Plan to visit Israel	33	83	76	83	41	NA	NA

*Variables are listed within each category from highest to lowest according to the general communal study averages.

nonaffiliated Jews and mixed-married households (about one-third). Weekly Sabbath attendance is about 40 percent for Jews, but higher for conversionary households (about two-thirds). About one-third of Jews light Sabbath candles, while almost half of our converts do so. Two measures of personal life observances—using kosher meat and keeping separate dishes for meat and milk—rate a low 20 percent for affiliated Jews, about 10 percent for converts, and fewer than 5 percent for nonaffiliates. As for religious commitment, fewer than half of Jews but two-thirds of converts belong to a congregation. As might be expected, households with a member of Christian origin tend to participate in Christmas and Easter rituals two-thirds of convert households observe Christmas, 95 percent of mixed-marriage households), but 13 percent of fully Jewish households also observe Christmas. The usual observance tends to be having a Christmas tree, giving gifts, and participating in a family gathering (rather than in a religious service).

In sum, the available data show conversionary households participating in religiously oriented practices at a slightly higher rate than born Jews in general but somewhat less than the religiously involved Jews in our study. At the same time conversionary households have more Christian practices in place than in-married Jews as a whole.

Ethnic Comparisons

Community involvement tends to be through a network of Jewish friends. For Jews, membership is lower than is contribution to Jewish organizations. Only about a third read Jewish press materials, participate in adult Jewish education, or visit Israel. As far as the data show, convert participation in Jewish organizational life is about the same as that of Jews as a whole.

Information on Jewish items in the household from previous studies was available only for conversionary and mixed marriages. The data clearly indicate a substantial level of Jewish items present in conversionary households (ranging from a high of 93 percent for a menorah to a low of 18 percent for separate dishes) as compared with mixed marriages (56 percent with a menorah to 7 percent with separate dishes).

What about more active forms of ethnic involvement? Egon Mayer has found that as a whole, Jews by choice scored higher than born Jews on religious behaviors but lower on their attitudes about

Jewish identification (1983, p. 62). Our study supports this finding. His conclusion is instructive: "Jews by choice are probably more adept at acting like Jews in matters of religious practices than they are at feeling or thinking like Jews when it comes to social relationships" (Mayer, 1983, p. 63).

Sandberg suggests that ethnic identification should be subdivided into (1) cultural, which involves knowledge about Jewish History, thought, and issues and (2) national, which includes participation in Jewish organizational activites, giving to support Jewish activities, and concern with the continuation of the Jewish community. How do the intermarried fair in these areas?

Table 4.12 shows some data on these ethnic aspects. In the Mayer data, conversionary marriages have patterns similar to religiously oriented born Jews; mixed marriages are considerably lower. Our converts evidence lower ethnic involvement than the Mayer group. Unfortunately, many issues that are important in understanding the ethnic dimension have not been measured in other studies. Attitudes toward the Holocaust and anti-Semitism, preference for Jewish foods, liking of Jewish jokes, understanding common Yiddish terms, knowledge about and preference for Jewish community services, and so on have not been measured. Other areas such as concern for Israel, the importance of helping Jews, and the importance of Jewish survival have been found by Mayer to be strong among intermarrieds, but comparative data are not provided (1985, p. 110). Certainly mixed-marrieds show a markedly decreased commitment to the survival of the Jewish community in succeeding generations. Only 25 percent of them want their children to identify as Jews (Mayer, 1987; see our Table 3.16.) Since two-thirds of intermarriages are mixed marriages, the Jewish community has reason to be concerned. However, conversionary marriages clearly come closer to the Jewish norm.

While hard data are lacking, observers point to the difficulty gentiles have in the area of ethnic assimilation. Sklare concludes:

> It is a sociological truth that although an individual may be converted to a faith he may remain outside of the group. The task of assimilating proselytes is relatively new for the Jewish community. . . . The born-Jew has a clear advantage over the convert through instrumentalities such as the nuclear family, the extended family and the all-Jewish clique group, he is provided with resources that help establish a Jewish commu-

nity. The proselyte does not have such avenues—if his [sic] identity is to grow, it is strongly dependent upon his own desires as well as those of his spouse. But it can not flourish in a vacuum—it must be supported by a community that desires to include him (1971, p. 208).

Since gentiles are accustomed to defining a religious identity in terms of church attendance, it is not surprising that converts more readily and frequently attach themselves to synagogue membership and participation (a Boston study found 57 percent of Jews by choice belonged to and attended a synagogue versus 39 percent of born Jews) (Silberman, 1985, p. 315). However, it appears that converts need greater assistance in becoming part of the community of Jews. In principle, the 1965 *Rabbi's Manual* of the Rabbinical Assembly indicates that "it is highly desirable that [the applicant] be introduced to Jewish families in order to affect as pleasant and easy a transition period as possible into the Jewish faith and the Jewish community," but in practice, no formalized mechanism is in place to ensure that this occurs.

Several converts have spoken about the difficulties they face in being accepted by the Jewish people (Levin, 1986; Kukoff, 1981). Unlike Christians who open their arms and doors in great warmth, concern, and support for converts, Jews are generally suspicious, often evidencing the attitudes quoted by Elchhorn: "Anyone who wants to become a Jew must either be insincere or unbalanced" (1965). Jews by choice are surprised and hurt by evidence of nonacceptance from Jews that continues for years. No matter that at least some converts know more about Judaism, participate in synagogue services more devotedly, and are more likely to continue their studies than most born Jews. After facing the fears and rejections of Christian friends, dealing with their own doubts, and making sincere efforts and commitments to Judalism and to being a Jew, the struggle that converts face in gaining full acceptance by Jews is more than some of them can handle. Often converts become more religious than their born Jewish spouses, which produces tension in their own households and with their Jewish in-laws. These are practical issues for converts and the Jewish community that are just beginning to be recognized.

We will return to a discussion of the community's role in Chapter 5. In the modern U. S. context, the community does have a legitimate concern about the stability of an intermarried relationship.

What does the research indicate about a culturally and religiously mixed couple's chance of building lasting marital bonds?

Stability of the Couple's Relationship

As we previously indicated, the traditional view was that intermarriage produced unstable, divorce-prone relationships. As Sklare observed, "Romantic love is fine, but it can be destroyed by incompatibilities that never before had occasion to rise to the surface or by ethic prejudices that partners were unaware of" (1971, p. 196).

Recent figures put the Jewish-gentile divorce rate at 55 percent, with the Jewish-Jewish rate at 10 percent (Gallob, 1985, p. 20). What kinds of conflicts do intermarrieds face that add stress to their relationship? As indicated in Chapter 1, negative reactions by Jewish in-laws, by Jewish leaders, and by the Jewish community may eventually take their toll (Gallob, March 6, 1986, p. 25; Gallob, September 25, 1986, p. 21). If children are born, further conflicts are likely over the education and identity of the children. Since most couples attempt a blended approach, they may find either the Christian or the Jewish relatives having a greater influence than they anticipated. Areas of potential conflict include the following:

Amount of involvement with Jews and with gentiles
Art
Communication styles
Foods
Health concerns
Holidays
Interest and concern about anti-Semitism
Interest in Israel
Interest in the Holocaust
Jokes
Life cycle events
Music
Parental contact
Political power concerns
Raising of children
Role beliefs

To overcome problems associated with these areas of potential disagreement, couples must work extra hard in their marriage and exercise considerable good will and tolerance. Certainly joint religious practices and community involvements can aid a couple's unity. Interestingly, our data showed more reported disagreements over religion among the in-married than the convert marriages. The five divorced converts who responded did not significantly differ from married converts.

SUMMARY OF COMPARISONS

The data presented in this chapter give us comparative information to put convert behavior into a realistic perspective. It also gives us a picture of the characteristics of the Jewish partner.

We found that the Jewish partners tended to be upper-middle-class professionals. They had very good relationships with their well-educated parents. They were exposed early to interacting with gentiles and had gentile friends in adolescence. They had on the average seven and one-half years of Jewish education, although they attended public school. A third remained religiously active as adults, 56 percent were satisfied with Judaism, two-thirds liked Jewish traditions. Fifty-seven percent of them identified with Reform Judaism. Half of their parents initially opposed their intermarriage, though their friends supported it. They disliked Christian services, and 98 percent of them and their parents favored conversion of their gentile partner. They did not view their potential in-laws as very religious, and 58 percent actively encouraged conversion of their mate.

Compared with in-married Jews, the Jewish partner had parents who were more positive toward gentiles. Both the Jewish partner and his gentile mate felt more positive toward his (Jewish) parents than toward his partner's parents, whom they saw less often as well. Surprisingly, our in-marrieds reported more disagreements at home than the out-marrieds.

In comparing converts, in-marrieds, and Jewish partners on their beliefs we found partners to be similar to in-married born Jews, with both dissimilar to the converts on adherence to Jewish, Christian, and ethnic-related beliefs. Converts were more likely to hold traditional Jewish beliefs than their Jewish partners or in-marrieds. Because traditional beliefs in being chosen, having a covenantal relationship with God, being a light to the nations, and expecting the Messiah are stressed in Christian teachings as the heritage that the Jewish people forsake, they are consequently well known to Christians even today.

At the same time, perhaps not surprisingly, converts held more Christian beliefs. Since, unlike Jews, converts tend to believe that Jesus never broke with Judaism, they don't feel a conflict in holding both Jewish and Christian beliefs. (It should be noted, though, that only 10 percent of converts strongly held Christian beliefs. The remainder adhered to a milder, more qualified version of Christian doctrines.)

Converts and Jews stress different ethnic beliefs. Converts seem more concerned with issues that immediately affect them, such as anti-Semitism, while Jews were more concerned with community survival, especially for Israel.

Students' views of what Jews believe did not change as a result of the introductory course. They correctly assess Jews' low adherence to Christian beliefs and high support for in-marriage. They underestimate our religiously involved Jews' holding of religious and especially of ethnic concerns, although the belief patterns attributed to Jews may be a better approximation of the general Jewish community that includes less involved Jews. They wrongly assess themselves as having stronger religious and ethnic beliefs than born-Jews, at least as represented by our study's born Jews.

Self-assessed knowledge of religious practices is similar for all three groups, but converts tend to believe they are more knowledgeable than their partners believe about themselves. Both converts and partners admit to less knowledge of Jewish community resources than did our in-married Jews.

In actual religious practices, our religiously oriented in-marrieds have the highest level of practice, then the Jewish partners, then the converts. However, in ethnic involvements the order tends to be in-marrieds, converts, and then partners. Apparently these converts do provide their household with vital links to the Jewish community that their partner might otherwise miss.

Of greatest concern to the future of the Jewish community is the fact that the convert and her partner share similarly weak views concerning the Jewish embeddedness of their children. They have less concern about their child or children having a Jewish identification, mostly Jewish friends, or a Jewish marital partner. They are also more tolerant of Christian exposures for their children than are in-marrieds, and they prefer that their children be free to choose their own religion.

Our data is generally similar to data from other studies. The partners in our study had more Jewish education, but that may be because other studies report all intermarriages whereas we are focusing on partners whose gentile spouses convert to Judaism. While our converts tend to have lower levels of practice than our religiously active born Jews, they do as well or better on major practices when compared with general Jewish population studies. This suggests that converts are making a needed contribution to the Jewish community. Their practice patterns are respectable when compared with the general Jewish community norms. It seems likely that while they do bring some Christian contacts into their Jewish household, converts also maintain a better than average religious connection and an average ethnic involvement. For conversionary couples, intermarriage appears to be a step into mainstream Judaism, not out of it.

Since we have now looked at the various kinds of information on converts that our study provides, we will turn our attention to making some recommendations based on those findings that we hope will help both potential and actual converts and the Jewish community. Chapter 5 presents that discussion.

5

Conclusions and Recommendations

WHAT CONCLUSIONS CAN one derive from the data and issues covered in our discussion? Is the issue of absorption versus assimilation an important consideration today? Should the Jewish community encourage conversion and, if so, under what conditions? Are there actions that would strengthen the integration of all converts and their children? What are the special needs of persons who convert on their own without a Jewish partner (15 percent in our convert study, 15 percent in a national 1984 study by Mayer, and 8 percent in our student groups)? What about those two-thirds of intermarrieds whose gentile partner does not convert? We now move from the data to what we view as appropriate conclusions.

CONCLUSIONS

There are no easy answers to these important questions that we have posed. On the surface it would appear that even though religion and family have lost most of their power to control behavior and that intermarriages are on the increase, the individual Jew maintains a high Jewish identity. According to Mayer (1987), even among the two-thirds of nonconversionary intermarrieds, 73 percent of Jewish partners retain their Jewish identity. That was not true in the past; for Jews who married gentiles, intermarriage often served as an opportunity to leave a community that was the object of hostility by the majority population and that imposed severe restrictions on Jewish ambitions in many areas of life. Today, though anti-Semitism is by no means eradicated, Jews by and large are not inhibited by their Jewishness and have attained recognition in most areas of American life. In addition, mainline churches, which in the past took every opportunity to convert Jews to Christianity, have now abandoned an organized "mission to Jews." Aggressive missionary efforts aimed at Jews are limited to a few fundamentalist Christian groups. American Jews are generally accepted, or at least tolerated, by the majority and secure and proud in their own identity. It would thus seem that we could conclude that U.S. Jews should have little concern about being assimilated by others and thus not be alarmed by intermarriage.

Actually, the absorption ability of the Jewish community requires more than personal security and a sense of pride in a Jewish identity. An intense commitment and energetic involvement is required by Jews if that identity is to be transmitted, otherwise Jewish life will be vulnerable to the forces of assimilation. As Kaplan stated, "When the contacts [between groups] result in inter-marriage, and children are born, the more vigorous civilization will be the one to which the children will belong" (1934/1957, p. 97). In fact the vital element of Jewish commitment is not a new consider-ation in the absorption/assimilation formula that we have posited. The strength of the Jewish community to absorb outsiders and its ability to resist attempts by others to overwhelm it have always come from an energetic, dynamic, and committed community. A convert joining such a community would absorb the commitment of the community and of his or her new Jewish in-laws.

What type of community and family is the convert joining today? Do the facts indicate a committed community and family or do they reveal a Jewish community with a minimal and superficial commit-ment?

Those who discourage conversion to Judaism argue that whereas it is true that currently Jewish identity in the United States seems to be secure and that there is a lessening of forces that formerly drove Jews away from the Jewish community, nevertheless that gain is offset by a weakening of commitment that is evident in contem-porary Jewish life. Consequently, the pessimists believe that the expectation that current converts can be absorbed by the Jewish community is not justified. From this view, the fragile identity of the modern Jewish community cannot withstand intermarriages. Who will be the role model for the convert? Pessimists can point to our study to bolster their argument that in a mostly weakly com-mitted Jewish community, converts would only further reflect and increase that weak commitment. To cite just a few discouraging examples from the data: 51 percent of the converts would not be concerned if their children married out of the faith/group; the extent of their knowledge about the Jewish community is minimal; only 17 percent report being regularly engaged in any form of adult Jewish education; and only 22 percent regularly attend synagogue Sabbath services. It would also be of concern that 80 percent of the converts are involved in secular aspects of Christmas, and as many as 10 percent retain some traditional Christian views even after conversion. These examples from our data certainly do not describe a group who would engage in the Jewish community's battle against assimilation but describe a group that would likely hasten its demise.

Others, more optimistically, can counter the above arguments by interpreting the Jewish condition and our data differently. We have ascertained, they would say, that Jews identify proudly with the Jewish community, which even by itself is an important commitment. Converts, they would say, not only reflect the standards of the general community, but at least some bring with them an even greater commitment. It is remarkable, they would argue, that after a rather short period of study, converts identify personally with the Jewish community. Though more than 80 percent began study attached to a Jewish partner, 82 percent considered themselves to be the prime initiators of their decision to convert. In many areas of religious observance they equal or surpass born Jews. They celebrate holidays in great numbers; for example, Hanukah (82 percent), Passover (85 percent), High Holiday services (80 percent), fasting on Yom Kippur (67 percent), Sabbath lighting of candles (47 percent), and recitation of *Kiddush* (34 percent); two-thirds belong to a synagogue, and 63 percent at least sometimes participate in Jewish adult education. Of course there is room for increasing involvement, but this represents a substantial beginning. Furthermore, what alternative is available to the Jewish community? It is either intermarriage without conversion or conversionary intermarriage. Intermarriage is an established fact that is unlikely to diminish in the free society in which we live. In fact the most recent data indicate a rise to more than 70 percent intermarriage for young Jews in major metropolitan centers (Gallob, 1988). The behavior of current converts as a group who receive minimal formal support is at least as good as that of born Jews as a group. Therefore, from a realistic point of view, the community can expect to maintain some stability and to decrease its losses if it encourages conversion and supports converts.

RECOMMENDATIONS

What are our recommendations based on our reading of the data and on our experience with converts and the conversion process? We propose that ways can and should be found to develop imaginative programs that will further strengthen converts' vital integration into the most active and committed segment of the Jewish community and that may help to draw greater numbers of intermarrieds to seek conversion. We make the following suggestions:

1. We call for the unconditional acceptance of the potential and actual convert by the Jewish family and by the Jewish community. Conversion is not to be looked upon as a compromise solution after all attempts have failed to discourage marriage between a Jew and a non-Jew. Our study shows that 46 percent of Jewish fathers and 47 percent of Jewish mothers are seen by the gentile partner as either disapproving of or neutral to the marriage of their child to a person who is willing to convert to Judaism; 18 percent of Jewish fathers and 14 percent of Jewish mothers are perceived as not supporting the conversion. Our data also showed that nonconverting gentile partners reported even more negative reactions. The message undoubtedly colors the family relationship from its very inception and discourages the non-Jew from commencing conversion studies, or, if they are undertaken, the potentially positive effects of the conversion may be reduced. Conversion, as we have indicated, in a short period of time places the convert on a par with the general Jewish community's practice and involvement. In the answers to our question "What do you like *least* about your experience with Jews and Judaism?" it became clear that the struggle to be fully accepted was a significant negative issue for the respondents. Almost a third of them perceived the Jewish community as generally negative toward converts and conversion. The following comments are instructive:

I don't like people who make their cutting remarks . . . "Oh, you wouldn't understand because you've converted" . . . who feel as if they need to keep you at arms' length.

I dislike that I will never be Jewish to some because I was not born a Jew.

Jews always think of me as a non-Jew or not a "real Jew."

How much more efficacious would their conversion be if these converts sense an enthusiastic welcome and support for their continuing education by the Jewish community and the Jewish family. How many are discouraged from converting because of such negative views? Jews need to understand that in the Christian community from which these people come, potential converts are lovingly wooed and supported, and those who convert are fully accepted, highly valued, and aided in numerous ways. Jews need help from the leadership level on down to confront their negative stereotypes and to develop more positive understandings about and approaches to drawing in intermarrieds in general and converts in particular. We call upon the community to develop sensitivity sessions between converts and born Jews, workshops, lectures, and other programs aimed at helping Jews become more positive toward these strangers in their midst. As Mayer points out, Jews are not very good in socializing outsiders:

> All minorities have difficulty being accepted as full-fledged equals in their host cultures, as we Jews, of all people, should know. This problem is all the more true for Jews by choice who must be integrated into Jewish culture and society which has not had the experience of integrating outsiders for nearly two thousand years (1983, p. 68).

2. While our data indicate that the Introduction to Judaism course is looked upon favorably by the converts, there is room for improvement. Many communities lack such organized efforts and should seek to establish them, using the Chicago course as a model. (However, our data indicate that the Chicago course itself could benefit from several changes, which we will discuss.) Besides participation by the potential convert, the Chicago course requires the Jewish partner to attend the class. The results have been gratifying and of significant help to the potential convert. By attending the same classes, partners are stimulated to discuss the issues and ideas raised and to develop a joint understanding. Through the course, Jewish partners often find new connections to Judaism that strengthen their own Jewish identity, commitment, and observance. One convert replying to our study appended a note saying, "My husband, who had attended Hebrew school, learned a tremendous amount in the class. He is more religious [now] due to our experience together in my conversion." Why not extend the class participation to include the parental Jewish family that the convert will join?

We also suggest that experiential sessions become an integral part of the course, such as a weekend retreat that could enable the group to exchange ideas and experiences on an informal basis, observe the Sabbath together, and interact in a joyous and meaningful setting. A group Sabbath experience could also encourage Sabbath and holiday attendance in students' synagogues. The class might also arrange group "field trips" to local synagogues to help students experience a variety of Jewish services within the various branches of Judaism. Such group worship experiences could be enhanced by prior discussion of the format and rituals they will see and by a postdiscussion of their observations, reactions, and questions. Group cultural trips could be an important addition as well.

From our data, introductory courses need to provide more discussion of the ethnic dimensions and issues for potential converts. Christians understand religious conversion but not ethnic integration, and thus they need guidelines to consider as they make changes in their lives. They need to have a better understanding of the tie between family rituals and the family closeness and unity of Jews that they are drawn to. Such understanding should help them incorporate and adapt Jewish home rituals, especially for Sabbath, into their family life. Sociological research on strong families clearly documents the value of home-centered rituals in developing family strength and unity. Frequent, regular family rituals are not just religiously important, they help stabilize families in an atomistic world such as ours.

More discussion of community concerns and reactions about intermarriage and conversion needs to be held so potential converts can understand the full context for the reactions they encounter, and so they can decide for themselves how best to address those concerns in their own lives. In particular, in a culture that stresses individual rights, discussion of issues concerning the needs and rights of the Jewish community should be explicitly addressed, especially as they relate to Christian beliefs, Christmas involvements, child Jewish socialization, and child friend/dating/marriage issues.

3. Committed members of the Jewish community, and preferably the immediate Jewish family if qualified in their commitment, should be recruited to serve as role models/mentors for intermarried and conversionary families. Currently without a systematic way of ensuring that non-Jews and converts are exposed to the best of Jewish traditions, their experiences are often counterproductive. For example, it is discouraging to teach the Introduction to Judaism course directed to potential converts on the week following the

Passover seder. Prior to the holiday they have studied the Passover *Haggadah* with its rituals and anticipated the forthcoming seder with all its rich symbolism, discussions of freedom, and warm fellowship; their expectation is to be uplifted spiritually. The impression gained from the seder is often quite the opposite of their anticipation. The leader conducting the seder is described as one "racing through the *Haggadah*." The family and guests, instead of discussing the meaning of freedom, are impatient for the meal, and the entire evening lacks spirituality. In truth, the actual seder has no resemblance to the seder they learned about in their studies. Their experience can be summarized by a parody in the play *Beau Jeste*, where the total ceremony is limited to the statement, "We were slaves, and we were freed; now let's eat." The community should seek authentic role models who would adopt a convert for at least a year. These knowledgeable families should invite converts and their spouses for Sabbath dinners, holiday celebrations, synagogue and community offerings, lectures, and social events.

Such an organized support effort could aid converts in becoming integrated into the life of the Jewish community and into the best of its home-oriented rituals. A people who want to perpetuate their future and thus assure their creative survival need to invest time and effort with new Jews and not force them to fend for themselves. The Jewish community has already developed imaginative programs for the integration of Soviet Jewry that are bearing fruit. Those programs could serve as models for similar support offered to potential and actual converts. It cannot be assumed that their Jewish partner or in-laws, if they have them, will be able to provide the intensive mentoring they need to firmly establish themselves as Jews. At the very most, intermarrieds have only one Jewish family to call on instead of two. For those without attachment to a Jewish partner, the need for a mentoring Jewish family is even stronger. And even nonconversionary intermarrieds could likely use some role models, perhaps other intermarrieds who have evidenced strong Jewish commitments. A systematic, well-organized program is required to truly absorb converts into the Jewish community. And to make the route less difficult and more supportive and attractive may well draw others of the two-thirds who presently do not convert.

4. Ongoing support programs should be made available for converts and their spouses. Paul and Rachael Cowen, the authors of *Mixed Blessings* (1987), have increased our awareness of the possible frictions that emerge periodically in a conversionary marriage,

particularly prior to Christmas-Hanukah and Easter-Passover, which evoke childhood memories and nostalgia. Our data also confirm that former beliefs do not necessarily disappear with conversion, so that one out of ten converts maintain major Christian beliefs, and the vast majority celebrate Christmas as a secular holiday. Some who answered our Study of Judaism Survey were frank in their responses. One wrote, "It is very difficult to completely abandon a religion you have grown up with." Another wrote, "Becoming a Jew and practicing as a Jew have been very overwhelming. . . . Judaism for me will only be my religion, and while [religion] is important, my identity as a Southerner will always be paramount." It is difficult for converts to erase their past. This can lead to creative infusions, as one convert remarked, "I enjoy taking the best aspects of my past traditions and incorporating them into a Jewish context. For example, when my daughter was named at Temple, she wore a beautiful gown, sort of like Christening. . . ." Or the difficulty in knowing what to adapt and what to delete can lead to less benign syncretizations, such as a "Hanukah bush" or to other problems for the conversionary household. We urge that the community provide a place for converts to ventilate their feelings and resolve the tensions inherent in a conversion process.

Former converts and their spouses could be recruited to act as "Big Buddies" to fledgling intermarrieds. Formal support networks should be organized among course participants rather than left to chance. Students should be told about the outreach and follow-up programs sponsored by Reform Judaism, and those programs should be expanded to Conservative converts.

A trained rabbi and a therapist should be available for individual and group counseling of converts and their families as needed. The time spent in discussing the dilemmas intermarrieds will face is, of necessity, very limited in any introductory course. Problems, doubts, and tensions often occur and reoccur after conversion. Rabbis and mental health workers can jointly formulate a program of counseling. The divorce rate is much higher for intermarriages (55 percent) than for in-marriages (10 percent). The community in such divorces stands to lose not only the convert but also the children. And "spiritual custody" battles do no one good. A nonthreatening, readily available counseling program could help intermarrieds understand that difficulties are the norm, are to be expected, and can be supportively handled.

A convert-oriented monthly or quarterly newsletter could be initiated at the local level to inform converts of relevant community programs and services and to discuss Jewish seasonal, ethnic, and other issues, to frankly face common problems experienced by converts, and to aid converts' knowledge, identity, and integration.

5. Synagogues have special obligations to aid in the integration of the convert. The initial contact of potential converts through the final ceremony of conversion is entrusted to the hands of the rabbinate. It is encouraging that our data show that 69 percent of converts are affiliated with the synagogue. This is a slightly higher percentage than the 60 percent for born Jews. Synagogues should undertake special efforts to increase the converts' appreciation of and involvement in Judaism. The synagogue should encourage converts to make up the life cycle events that they have missed. Some life cycle events are required of converts as part of the conversion process; for example, basic studies in Judaism, circumcision or *hatafat dam brit,* immersion, and taking a Hebrew name. However, we suggest that other life cycle events should also be encouraged for converts, such as a public naming and conversion recognition ceremony, the public naming and dedication of any children in the relationship, a reaffirmation in a Jewish marriage ceremony for one that took place prior to conversion, and the *bar* or *bat mitzvah.* These events could become community celebrations. Not only could participation make up for Jewish life cycle events that were missed, but it would also provide additional years of study and serve as a message that the synagogue values its converts and wants to help them be involved in greater participation in the religious, cultural, and social life of the synagogue and to deepen their religious commitment. The synagogue should provide classes for converts to learn Hebrew, the prayers, the daily service, holiday services, and home rituals. Besides religiously oriented instruction, classes for learning common Jewish songs, dances, stories, games, and even jokes that are taught to children could be initiated for converts. Cooking classes focusing on recipes for the major holidays are another resource that converts could utilize.

Such classes could be of use to born Jews as well as to converts, thus making them viable for synagogues with small numbers of converts. In communities where individual synagogues cannot afford to provide these supports, classes could be jointly or centrally run instead.

6. We suggest that the continuing education of the convert be-

come the responsibility of the organized Jewish community. The conversion ceremony should be viewed not as the culmination of the Jewish experience but as its beginning. It is true that Hillel, a rabbi often quoted in the Talmud, participated in the conversion of a proselyte who wished to know all about Judaism while standing on one foot, but even Hillel, who summarized the essence of Judaism in his famous statement, "What is distasteful to you do not do to others," added, "The rest is commentary, now go and study." In the Jewish tradition, the very rituals of conversion, such as circumcision and immersion in water, signify that converts become newly born. The message of the tradition is that a proselyte is a neophyte in the understanding of Judaism and, like any child, is called upon to increase his or her knowledge.

An organized program of ongoing Jewish studies and reading should be made readily available. A variety of learning formats should be developed on topics such as the prayers, the services, the Passover rituals, traditional religious and ethnic music, Jewish history, Jewish humor, and current issues. Some examples of learning aids are instructional tapes, video programs such as "Civilization and the Jews" and "When Love Meets Tradition" (developed by the Reform branch), mail-in study programs, or at least bibliographies and resource information sheets on relevant topics. Some of this material is already available, but converts need to become aware of it and provided easy access, and some new material needs developing. Perhaps synagogue or Jewish community center libraries could be expanded to include such resources for loan.

A year's tuition scholarship to Spertus College of Judaica or its equivalent could be paid by the Jewish community. Besides a tuition scholarship for some, a Jewish magazine gift subscription could be given to all participants in the introductory course. A local Jewish publication such as *The Sentinel* and/or a national Jewish magazine such as *Moment* could be most helpful in aiding the converts' understanding and knowledge about Jewish life. They would sense by reading the periodical both the dynamism of Jewish life and its resources—its debates, its news, its cultural activities, its bookstores, its restaurants, and so on.

There needs to be some effort at investigating why such a large number of converts acknowledge the importance of and their interest in continuing their Jewish education, but so few (17 percent) regularly do so. Efforts can then be more clearly directed at overcoming those obstacles. Such supportive measures would go a long way to help converts learn about the Jewish community and to partake of its resources and issues. Even considered on practical grounds, a modest investment could reap large dividends for the community in encouraging the involvement of converts in its life. A recent "Book of Life," a publication of the Chicago Jewish Federation indicating the annual monetary gifts to the Jewish United Fund, contains the names of Soviet Jews who made significant contributions only a few years after settling in Chicago. These people were helped by the Federation to immigrate and settle in the area. To show their appreciation, the new Jewish Americans have become contributors to the Federation's fund-raising campaigns.

7. For a limited time after their conversion (say three to five years) it would be wise to consider converts a distinct group entitled to preferential and supportive treatment. We are well aware of the admonition in the Jewish tradition that one is prohibited from reminding a convert of her or his former status and that one must not differentiate between a born Jew and a proselyte. This policy was established to prevent negative discrimination and second-class citizenship for converts. Rather, we propose positive, special treatment as a kind of "internship" in Judaism. To encourage the ethnic identification of converts, we suggest special "convert missions to Israel" to enable them to spend meaningful time in a totally Jewish setting and thereby deepen their Jewish identity. Jews themselves have had enough experience to know the value to the community, both spiritually and financially, of people touched by Israel through their participation in missions. If convert-only missions cannot be offered, then converts could be given subsidies in order to participate in trips to Israel organized by other groups from the community.

Those applying for the subsidies could be required to pursue a study program prior to their departure for Israel. We envision six months of weekly preparatory classes to qualify for the mission. Lectures on the history of ancient Israel, Zionism, and modern Israel and a taste of the *ulpan* method for studying the Hebrew language would enhance converts' appreciation of Israel. Such classes could be open even to those unable to actually travel to Israel and to born Jews as well. Non-traveling participants could receive reports and see pictures from the travelers' experiences to stimulate them vicariously. We are aware that not everyone would participate in such programs, but those who did would be immensely enriched,

and, in the long run, the Jewish community would be the benefici-
ary.

Locally, special federation mini-missions could be run to introduce potential and new converts to community resources and programs. The Chicago Federation has organized successful mini-
missions for rabbis, elected board members of the Federation, contributors, and others. Why not a "mini-mission" for new Jews? The
community can point to its many activities with pride; why keep
them a secret from Jews by choice? The support given to the Jewish
centers, educational networks, programs for the aged, aid to the
poor, and family counseling services could be made part of the
awareness of new Jews by direct experience. Jewish networks would
be expanded for those joining the community.

It must be kept in mind that these young professional families
tend not to live in highly Jewish areas. Consequently, programs to
help them develop ethnic awareness, identifications, and networks
need to be planned, perhaps as part of ongoing "refresher" or follow-
up postcourse group events. In addition, those converts without
partners (10 percent to 20 percent) need help to enter the Jewish
singles scene and the aid of "matchmakers," since most people meet
their spouse through friend and family introductions.

8. Children of out-marriages require special attention. Our
study, though limited because of the age of the children, points to
potentially disturbing facts. It is understandable that converts
would find it difficult to send a message to their children that they
would oppose intermarriage or that they would stand in the way of
a child's choice of religion. We found that 79 percent of converts
would encourage their children to make their own choice of religion,
83 percent are certain they would not restrict their children's dating
to Jews (another 14 percent are unsure; only 3 percent indicate they
actually plan on restrictions), and 72 percent believe that restrictions are not important. If the message that they should embrace
Judaism and marry a Jew can't come decisively from the parents,
should it not come from the Jewish community?

The Jewish community must find ways to deepen the Jewish
identity and commitment of children of conversionary marriages.
We suggest that scholarships be made available to children of
converts for attendance at Jewish day schools, Jewish camps, and a
junior year in Israel. The community should do no less for the
children of converts than it already does for children of Russian
immigrants who currently are granted scholarships to day schools

and camps. The convert and the conversionary family are also recent "arrivals" to the Jewish community.

The introductory course should be organized to spend explicit time on issues concerning how to raise a Jewish child. Our data show that this concern is not addressed and that converts do not increase their commitments to Jewish child-rearing over the course of study or in comparison with nonconverts. Discussion should be planned about issues of Jewish survival and transmission of identity, the importance and handling of friend and dating relationships, and the conflicts between tolerance of other groups and of inmarriage requirements. Because of the complexities of the issues, ongoing seminars, workshops, and discussion groups on child-rearing issues for various ages of children need to be offered by the community. Born Jews are just as likely to benefit from these kinds of parental supports and should be invited as well to share their struggles and successes.

Volunteer Jewish grandfathers and grandmothers might provide helpful, secondary inputs, models, and supports to conversionary children in their impressionable seven- to sixteen-year-old years. Like born Jews, conversionary family children would then have two sets of Jewish grandparents from whom to learn stories, traditions, and attitudes.

9. Converts can be asked to serve as a bridge to the non-Jewish community. Obviously because of their circle of non-Jewish friends and family they are in a position to become ambassadors of good will in the general community and thus help break down the stereotypes about Jews that are still prevalent. Rabbis have found converts to be effective in many such areas. Quite recently, in an experience with a school system, a particularly recalcitrant teacher failed to recognize the distress of Jewish parents when he demanded that a major examination be given on Yom Kippur. An indignant convert, without the baggage of self-consciousness that many Jews carry, demanded the postponement of tests on religious grounds. What the Jewish community couldn't do, she accomplished in one session with the principal, and the matter was settled in an amicable fashion. We suggest that in areas of public relations, interdenominational activities, and Israel concerns, converts' active presence and leadership should be sought.

Converts can also be asked to lead discussions on Christianity and Christian perspectives to inform the Jewish community. Jews themselves often hold false views of Christian doctrines, concerns, and issues and are unaware of the diversity within Christianity or of changes in Christian attitudes and teachings about Jews. Converts could be helpful in working with junior high and high school Jewish children to help them understand the important differences between Christians and Jews, to discuss how to answer Christian missionaries, and to share the value of choosing to be a Jew.

10. Finally, we suggest that the Shavuot holiday commemorating the Sinaitic revelation and the proclamation of the Ten Commandments be established as a day for honoring the thousands of Jews by choice who have joined the Jewish fold. The Jewish community should not overlook the element of heroism and risk it takes for one to convert to Judaism in the twentieth century. A person living in the century of the Holocaust surely is aware that to become a Jew is to join a community that is vulnerable to discrimination and persecution and thus deserves recognition for that courageous act.

The festival of Shavuot, with its emphasis on Jews' receiving the Torah for the first time and the traditional reading of the book of Ruth, the classic convert to Judaism, would be the logical and appropriate place for such tributes to Jews by choice. A new ritual could be developed such as calling only Jews by choice to the Torah, having converts read from the book of Ruth, having the service including the sermon be handled by conversionary intermarrieds, and having converts relate their Jewish experiences. Such a ceremony could enhance converts' acceptance and lift the morale of the congregants.

Having made these recommendations, it should be apparent that we, as the authors of the study, believe that a deeper commitment on the part of the Jewish community to its own religious spirituality and its institutions would reflect itself in a greater commitment by Jews by choice. Should we aggressively seek to convert gentiles to Judaism? Our opinion is that we should continue to revere the saying of Hillel, "What is distasteful to you do not do to others." Jews have always been uncomfortable with those who wished to convert them to other faiths. That discomfort turned to anger when missionaries proclaimed that "there is no salvation outside the church." No such doctrine exists in Judaism. On the contrary, less is required to attain salvation for a gentile than it is for a Jew. According to rabbinic tradition, a Jew is obligated to observe 613 commandments; a non-Jew is required to observe only seven Noachide Laws (*Sanhedrin* 56–60; Genesis, Chapter 9). These laws are mainly in the moral sphere—avoiding bloodshed, sexual sins, theft, cruelty to animals, idolatry, and blasphemy, and establishing a legal system. Maimonides taught that one who observes these laws has a share in the world to come even without becoming a Jew and is entitled to the highest earthly honors (*Encyclopedia Judaica*, 1956, p. 358). However, if a gentile wishes to become a Jew, the doors should always be open without reservations and the community should warmly accept Jews by choice. As in the time of the Second Commonwealth, gentiles should be attracted to Judaism because of the enthusiastic involvement and excitement about Jewish life exhibited by Jews themselves. Certainly the option of conversion should be discussed with the gentile by the Jewish partner and by the potential in-laws, but the discussion should be without coercion. If an intermarriage does occur without conversion, as much support as possible for a Jewish life-style should be afforded those couples who comprise two-thirds of the intermarrieds. And the door should remain open for conversion at a later time. Mayer's data (1987) and ours both indicate that of the one-third of intermarrieds who currently convert, one-fourth do so only after the birth of their first child, and another fourth even later, usually before the child's *bar* or *bat mitzvah*.

Thus far, our recommendations have been directed to the Jewish community. We are aware that the suggestions we've made can be implemented on a piece-meal and partial basis or, worse, not at all, by each Jewish community. However, we believe the current situation warrants central planning and coordination. The Reform movement has already established a commission on outreach directed by Lydia Kukoff, herself a convert. That commission, along with local outreach efforts, has already begun to develop some materials and programs along the lines we have suggested. We call on all segments of Judaism to cooperate in developing the work done by Reform outreach. They certainly have seen a payoff from the limited efforts they have made thus far, since the majority of converts are to Reform Judaism. We hope our work will give impetus to a stronger cooperative effort using the model of Reform outreach and of Federation-sponsored programs for Soviet Jews. Much of what we've recommended would benefit born Jews, if they were invited to participate (as they should be), as well as intermarrieds and converts. Recently Tobin, who has researched and written about intermarriage for some time, made a number of suggestions for strengthening the commitment and viability of born Jews as a method of influencing the rates of out-marriage without conversion. He concluded, "A vital

Judaism can thrive in the openness of American society if we light Shabbat candles, not Yahrzeit candles in the face of intermarriage" (1990, p. 63). The programs we suggest are in keeping with his recommendations for actions to increase the value of Judaism and the Jewish experience for born Jews.

Finally, we want to address a few remarks to potential and actual converts to Judaism. The process of becoming a Jew is a process of resocialization, not just learning a few new religious holiday rituals. Converts indicate that even in the religious realm, major changes in life-style and beliefs are required. In addition, the ethnic dimension, "feeling, talking, reacting like a Jew," and being accepted as a Jew by Jews, takes even more time and effort. A commitment to lifelong study and involvement must be made and followed through. The potential convert would also be wise to heed the advice of one who went through the process and who made the following statement in the questionnaire returned to us:

Make sure that you are converting for yourself and not a mate or a future mate. It is very hard to be a Jew, and you need a real commitment to be a Jew by choice. . . . Remember you have gone down a very difficult road to get where you are . . . search your soul.

It is our opinion that to become Jewish in order to have a unified household is a legitimate first step, but as Hillel said to the gentile, *"V'iduch zil gmor,"* ("The rest go and study"). That rest of Judaism must be acquired through intensified emotional and rational study. And raising Jewishly committed children who will marry a Jew or convert to Judaism is the ultimate proof of the seriousness and effectiveness of that commitment. Only then can the convert, a Jew by choice, truly say, "Your people are my people, and your God is my God," and the Jewish community will answer, "Amen."

Appendix: Supplemental Tables for Chapter 4

TABLE 4.3

COMPARISONS AMONG BORN JEWS' (BJ), PARTNERS' (PR), AND CONVERTS' (CV) BACKGROUND PUSH FACTORS

Push Variables	Means			Significant Differences*		
	Born Jews	Partners	Converts	BJ vs. PR	BJ vs. CV	PR vs. CV
Sex	0.54	0.27	0.80			+
Age	47.45	33.35	35.17	−	−	
Adolescent Relationship to Father	3.27	3.10	2.68			−
Adolescent Relationship to Mother	3.34	3.40	2.95		−	−
Father's View of Jews	4.42	4.26	2.44		−	−
Mother's View of Jews	4.32	4.32	2.55		−	−
Father's View of Gentiles	2.60	2.76	NA	+		
Mother's View of Gentiles	2.27	2.76	NA	+		
Father's Gentile Friends	2.41	2.67	NA	+		
Mother's Gentile Friends	2.18	2.67	NA	+		

Father's Religious Activity	2.33	2.26	1.95			
Mother's Religious Activity	1.93	2.19	2.61		+	+
Childhood Religious Involvement	2.50	2.64	3.14		+	+
Years of Formal Religious Instruction	2.48	7.62	7.05	+	+	+
Years of Formal Religious School	1.10	1.06	2.86		+	+
Dissatisfaction with Childhood Religion	2.56	2.56	1.29		−	−
Adult View about Jesus as Divine	0.76	0.93	1.29		+	+
Total, Questioning about God**	10.48	10.13	11.44	+	+	+
Total, Childhood Major Rabbinic Religious Practices**	6.35	7.23	NA	−		
Total, Childhood Supportive Rabbinic Religious Practices**	5.50	6.14	NA	+		
Total, Childhood Christian Practices**	1.42	1.97	NA	+		
Total, Childhood Knowledge of Primary Blessings**	2.92	3.41	NA	+		
Total, Childhood Ethnic Inputs**	1.93	2.35	NA	+		

* "−" indicates that the comparision score is significantly lower than the born Jews' score; in the case of PR vs. CV, partners represent born Jews.

"+" indicates that the comparison score is significantly higher than the born Jews' score; in the case of PR vs. CV, partners represent born Jews.

** A description of the Total (scale) variables can be obtained from Dr. Forster.

TABLE 4.4
COMPARISONS AMONG BORN JEWS' (BJ), PARTNERS' (PR), AND CONVERTS' (CV) BACKGROUND PULL FACTORS

	Means			Significant Differences*		
Pull Variables	Born Jews	Partners	Converts	BJ vs. PR	BJ vs. CV	PR vs. CV
Partner's Family Relationship Compared with Own						
Family	NA	0.80	1.49			+
Get Along with Partner's Father	3.34	1.06	1.08	–	–	
Get Along with Partner's Mother	2.75	0.91	0.97	–	–	
See Partner's Family	3.44	2.99	3.46	–		+
See Own Family	3.78	3.61	3.39		–	–
Disagree with Partner	2.41	2.01	2.06	–	–	
Considered Converting to Christianity	0.11	0.09	NA			
Belief That Conversion Is Important to Be Part of the						
Jewish Community	NA	3.42	3.84			+

Converts Accepted by Jews	3.62	3.41	2.93		−	−
Converts Are Serious About Being a Jew	2.51	2.56	NA			
Converts Are Observant	2.24	2.25	NA			
Converts Are Observant as Jews	2.24	2.74	2.60	+	+	+
Converts Are Involved in the Jewish Community	2.13	2.05	NA			
Converts Are as Active as Jews	2.29	2.50	2.07			
Difficulty in Being a Convert	0.89	0.82	1.99		−	−
Difficulty in Being a Jew	1.53	1.53	NA		+	+
Converts Contribute to Judaism	3.22	3.49	3.28	+		−
Like Converts	4.38	4.70	NA	+		
Jews Understand Converts	2.72	2.17	2.58	−		
Rabbi Supports Converts	4.83	4.74	4.81			
A Jewish Identity Is Personally Important	3.73	3.62	3.04			

* "—" indicates that the comparison score is significantly lower than the born Jews' score; in the case of PR vs CV, partners represent born Jews.

"+" indicates that the comparison score is significantly higher than the born Jews' score; in the case of PR vs. CV, partners represent born Jews.

TABLE 4.5

COMPARISONS AMONG BORN JEWS' (BJ), PARTNERS' (PR), AND CONVERTS' (CV) BELIEF PATTERNS

Belief Variables**	Means			Significant Differences*		
	Born Jews	Partners	Converts	BJ vs. PR	BJ vs. CV	PR vs. CV
General Religious Beliefs						
Often Talk About Religion	2.44(1)	1.64(6)	1.93(5)	−	−	
Frequently Feel Close to God	2.23(2)	2.57(1)	2.62(1)		+	
Prayer Is Important	1.90(3)	1.80(4)	2.39(4)		+	+
Believe in God as Father	1.87(4)	2.22(3)	2.50(2)	+	+	
Religion Influences Daily Life	1.82(5)	1.72(5)	1.57(6)			−
Experience Presence of Divine in Life	1.70(6)	2.54(2)	2.40(3)	+	+	
Jewish Religious Beliefs						
Humans Have Free Will to Choose Good	3.43(1)	2.69(6)	3.44(1)	−		+
Judaism Has More Truth Than Other Religions	3.32(2)	2.94(4)	3.15(3)	−		
There Is Only One God	2.75(3)	3.03(3)	3.24(2)	+	+	+
Beliefs Don't Matter, A Moral Life Does	2.64(4)	2.25(9)	2.44(9)			
Jesus' Messiahship Was a Creation of the Early Church	2.59(5)	4.34(1)	2.46(8)	+		−
God Promised the Land of Israel to the Jews	2.47(6)	3.30(2)	2.67(6)	+		
Jews Have a Covenantal Relationship with God	2.46(7)	2.66(7)	2.89(4)		+	
Rabbinic Interpretations Are Valid	2.04(8)	2.38(8)	2.64(5)		+	
Jews Are Chosen to Be a Light to the Nations	1.99(9)	2.04(10)	2.19(10)		+	
The Hebrew Bible is God's Revealed Word	1.78(10)	2.70(5)	2.51(7)		+	
Moral Non-Jews Will Be Saved	1.71(11)	1.87(11)	2.16(11)		+	+
God Will Send the Messiah at Time's End	1.61(12)	1.83(12)	1.94(12)			
Total, Acceptance of Major Rabbinical Beliefs*	29.09	29.57	31.02			

	In-married Born Jews					
Christian Religious Beliefs						
Jesus Broke with Judaism	2.44(1)	3.97(1)	2.40(1)	+	+	−
Jesus Will Return as Messiah	0.57(2)	0.58(4)	1.10(3)		+	+
God Exists as a Trinity	0.49(3)	0.39(6)	1.05(5)		+	+
Jesus Rose from the Dead	0.42(4)	0.40(5)	1.07(4)		+	+
God Revealed Himself in Jesus	0.40(5)	0.90(2)	1.17(2)		+	+
The Resurrection Proves Jesus Was the Messiah	0.36(6)	0.79(3)	0.78(6)		+	
Total, Acceptance of Major Christian Beliefs#	2.15	2.17	4.06		+	+
Jewish Ethnic Beliefs						
Feel a Bond to Israel	3.85(1)	3.15(3)	2.48(11)		−	−
There Must Always Be a Jewish People	3.80(2)	2.90(7)	3.55(1)		−	−
The U.S. Should Aid Israel	3.64(3)	2.81(8)	2.98(7)		−	−
Being Jewish Is Personally Important	3.61(4)	3.60(1)	3.22(3)	−	−	−
Want to Be Part of the Jewish Community	3.57(5)	3.26(2)	3.04(5)		−	−
Anti-Semitism Is a Problem in the U.S.	3.54(6)	2.72(11)	3.28(2)		−	−
It Is Important to Vote for Politicians Who Support Israel	3.44(7)	3.09(5)	2.74(9)		−	−
Feel Comfortable in Jewish Settings	3.37(8)	2.52(12)	3.02(6)		−	−
Feel Obliged to Help World Jewry	3.36(9)	3.08(6)	2.94(8)	−		−
Have Satisfying Life Goals	3.11(10)	2.80(9)	3.14(4)	−	−	
Jewish Parents Should Make Sure Their Kids Don't Marry Non-Jews	2.97(11)	1.55(13)	1.42(13)			−
The Press is Too Negative about Israel	2.66(12)	2.74(10)	2.18(13)		−	−
The Synagogue Should Help Minorities	1.87(13)	3.10(4)	2.51(10)		+	+
Total, Major Ethnic Involvement Beliefs#	24.26	21.87	20.11	−	−	−

* "−" indicates that the comparison score is significantly lower than the born Jews' score; in the case of PR vs. CV, partners represent born Jews.

* "+" indicates that the comparison score is significantly higher than the born Jews' score; in the case of PR vs. CV, partners represent born Jews.

** Variables are listed within each category from highest to lowest according to the in-married, born Jew mean; bracketed number (for example, (1)) is the rank.

\# A description of the Total (scale) variables can be obtained from Dr. Forster.

TABLE 4.6

COMPARISONS AMONG STUDENT PERCEPTIONS OF JEWISH BELIEFS (PJ), STUDENTS' OWN BELIEFS (ST), AND ACTUAL BELIEFS OF PARTNERS (PR) AND BORN JEWS (BJ)

Belief Variables**	Student Perception of Jewish Beliefs*	Actual Beliefs			Significant Differences*		
		Born Jews	Partners	Students	PJ vs. BJ	PJ vs. PR	PJ vs. ST
General Religious Beliefs							
Frequently Feel Close to God	2.19(1)	2.23(2)	2.57(1)	2.74(1)		+	+
Prayer Is Important	2.11(2)	1.90(3)	1.80(4)	2.07(3)		−	−
Believe in God as Father	2.07(3)	1.87(4)	2.22(3)	2.11(4)	−	+	+
Often Talk about Religion	1.90(4)	2.44(1)	1.64(6)	1.64(5)	+	−	−
Experience Presence of Divine in Life	1.77(5)	1.70(6)	2.54(2)	2.52(2)		+	+
Religion Influences Daily Life	1.00(6)	1.82(5)	1.72(5)	1.61(6)	+	+	+
Jewish Religious Beliefs							
Judaism Has More Truth than Other Religions	2.77(1)	3.32(2)	2.94(4)	3.22(6)	+	+	+
There Is Only One God	2.67(2)	2.75(3)	3.03(3)	3.20(7)		+	+
Jews Have a Covenantal Relationship with God	2.63(3)	2.46(7)	2.66(7)	3.07(8)	−		+
God Promised the Land of Israel to the Jews	2.63(4)	2.47(6)	3.30(2)	3.55(3)	−	+	+
Humans Have Free Will to Choose God	2.45(5)	3.43(1)	2.69(6)	2.67(10)	+	+	+
Rabbinic Interpretations Are Valid	2.36(6)	2.04(8)	2.38(8)	2.64(11)	−		+
The Hebrew Bible Is God's Revealed Word	2.28(7)	1.78(10)	2.70(5)	2.94(9)	−	+	+
Jews Are Chosen to Be a Light to the Nations	2.08(8)	1.99(2)	2.04(10)	3.39(5)			+
Jesus' Messiahship was a Creation of the Early Church	2.03(9)	2.59(5)	4.34(1)	3.52(4)	+	+	+
God Will Send the Messiah at Time's End	1.97(10)	1.61(12)	1.83(12)	4.34(1)	−	+	+

Beliefs Don't Matter, a Moral Life Does	1.79(11)	2.64(4)	2.25(9)	2.05(12)	+		+	+
Moral Non-Jews Will Be Saved	1.60(12)	1.71(11)	1.87(11)	3.93(2)		+	+	+
Christian Religious Beliefs								
Jesus Broke with Judaism	1.76(1)	2.44(1)	3.97(1)	3.37(1)	+		+	+
Jesus Will Return as Messiah	0.43(2)	0.57(2)	0.58(4)	2.30(4)				+
God Exists as a Trinity	0.39(3)	0.49(3)	0.39(6)	1.72(6)				+
God Revealed Himself in Jesus	0.27(4)	0.40(5)	0.90(2)	2.70(3)		+	+	+
Jesus Rose from the Dead	0.13(5)	0.42(4)	0.40(5)	2.14(5)	+	+	+	+
The Resurrection Proves Jesus Was the Messiah	0.10(6)	0.36(6)	0.79(3)	3.37(2)	+	+	+	+
Jewish Ethnic Beliefs								
Being Jewish Is Personally Important	2.80(1)	3.61(4)	3.60(1)	2.91(5)	+	+		
There Must Always Be Jewish People	2.80(2)	3.80(2)	2.90(7)	2.82(7)	+			
Want to Be Part of the Jewish Community	2.67(3)	3.57(5)	3.26(2)	2.69(8)	+			
Anti-Semitism Is a Problem in the U.S.	2.66(4)	3.54(6)	2.72(11)	2.59(9)	+			
The U.S. Should Aid Israel	2.63(5)	3.64(3)	2.81(8)	3.06(2)	+	+	+	+
Feel Obliged to Help World Jewry	2.58(6)	3.36(9)	3.08(6)	2.90(6)	+	+	+	+
Feel Comfortable in Jewish Settings	2.56(7)	3.37(8)	2.52(12)	2.57(10)	+			
It Is Important to Vote for Politicians Who Support Israel	2.55(8)	3.44(7)	3.09(5)	3.12(1)	+	+	+	+
Have Satisfying Life Goals	2.32(9)	3.11(10)	2.80(9)	2.61(11)	+	+	+	+
The Press Is Too Negative about Israel	2.08(10)	2.66(12)	2.74(10)	3.01(3)	+	+	+	+
Jewish Parents Should Make Sure Their Kids Don't Marry Non-Jews	2.05(11)	2.97(11)	1.55(13)	1.29(13)	+	−		−
The Synagogue Should Help Minorities	1.86(12)	1.87(13)	3.10(4)	3.00(4)			+	+
Feel a Bond to Israel	0.65(13)	3.85(1)	3.15(3)	1.78(12)	+	+	+	+

* "−" indicates that the comparison actual belief score is significantly lower than the perceived Jewish belief score.
+ "+" indicates that the comparison actual belief score is significantly higher than the perceived Jewish belief score.
** Variables are listed within each category from highest to lowest according to the perceived Jewish belief scores; bracketed number (for example, (1)) is the rank.
# Post-course and post-only course data used for students' perceived and own beliefs.

TABLE 4.7
COMPARISONS AMONG BORN JEWS' (BJ), PARTNERS' (PR), AND CONVERTS' (CV) KNOWLEDGE

Knowledge Variables**	Means			Significant Differences*		
	Born Jews	Partners	Converts	BJ vs. PR	BJ vs. CV	PR vs. CV
Jewish Religious Beliefs						
Jewish View of God	2.42(1)	2.56(1)	2.80(1)		+	+
Controversy on Who is a Jew	2.37(2)	2.40(2)	2.58(2)		+	
Conservative Judaism	2.17(3)	1.99(6)	2.16(6)	−		+
Orthodox Judaism	2.03(4)	1.89(7)	1.95(8)	−		
View of Jesus	2.01(5)	2.09(4)	2.47(3)		+	+
View of Christianity	1.98(6)	2.06(5)	2.35(4)		+	
Reform Judaism	1.96(7)	2.10(3)	2.35(5)		+	
The Talmud	1.47(8)	1.63(8)	2.00(7)		+	+
Jewish Practice Requirements						
Passover Seder	3.28(1)	3.05(1)	3.13(1)	−		
Yom Kippur Observance	3.17(2)	2.97(2)	3.03(2)	−		
Sabbath Observance	2.89(3)	2.75(3)	2.87(3)			
Sitting *Shiva*—Mourning	2.82(4)	2.54(4)	2.57(5)	−	−	
Brit Milah—Circumcision	2.69(5)	2.33(7)	2.74(4)	−		+
Kosher Home	2.68(6)	2.34(6)	2.41(8)			
Kashrut—Dietary Laws	2.66(7)	2.38(5)	2.45(7)			
Sukkot	2.30(8)	2.08(9)	2.15(10)	−		+
Expected Mitzvot	2.00(9)	2.17(8)	2.56(6)		+	+
Daily Worship	1.97(10)	1.99(10)	1.94(11)			
Mikvah—Family Purity	1.56(11)	1.56(11)	2.21(9)		+	+
Total, Knowledge of Major Rabbinic Practice Requirements*	26.97	25.59	27.07	−	−	−
Total, Knowledge of Primary Jewish Blessings*	3.47	3.57	2.69		+	−

Jewish History and Issues						
Shoah (Holocaust)	3.22(1)	3.05(1)	3.19(1)	−	−	+
Zionism	2.65(2)	2.34(2)	2.32(3)	−	−	
Biblical History	2.51(3)	2.34(3)	2.44(2)	−		
Postbiblical History	2.50(4)	2.29(4)	2.30(4)	−	−	
Jewish Community Resources						
The Sentinel	3.35(1)	2.47(4)	2.06(6)	−	−	+
Jewish Community Centers	3.00(2)	2.80(1)	2.62(3)	−	−	
The Ark	2.82(3)	1.98(7)	2.17(5)	−	−	
Spertus College of Judaica	2.81(4)	2.78(2)	3.29(1)	+	+	
Michael Reese Hospital	2.78(5)	2.69(3)	2.96(2)	−	−	
Jewish Vocational Service	2.74(6)	2.07(6)	1.76(9)	−		
Mount Sinai Hospital	2.58(7)	2.42(5)	2.44(4)			
Council for Jewish Elderly	2.48(8)	1.97(8)	1.88(7)	−		
Board of Jewish Education	2.43(9)	1.85(9)	1.58(10)	−		
Jewish Family and Community Services	2.34(10)	1.81(10)	1.86(8)	−		
Jewish Children's Bureau	2.34(11)	1.60(11)	1.52(11)	−		
Hebrew Theological College	2.15(12)	1.54(12)	1.36(12)	−		
Drexel Home	2.09(13)	1.22(13)	0.87(13)	−	−	
Response Center	1.26(14)	1.00(15)	0.72(15)	−		
Associated Talmud Torahs	1.67(15)	1.11(14)	0.80(14)	−		
Total, Knowledge of Major Jewish Agencies*	37.01	29.23	27.59	−	−	

* "−" indicates that the comparison score is significantly lower than the born Jews' score; in the case of PR vs. CV, partners represent born Jews.

"+" indicates that the comparison score is significantly higher than the born Jews' score; in the case of PR vs. CV, partners represent born Jews.

** Variables are listed within each category from highest to lowest according to the in-married, born Jew mean; bracketed number (for example, (1)) is the rank.

\# A description of the Total (scale) variables can be obtained from Dr. Forster.

TABLE 4.8
COMPARISONS AMONG BORN JEWS' (BJ), PARTNERS' (PR), AND CONVERTS' (CV)
PATTERNS OF REGULAR JEWISH RELIGIOUS PRACTICES

	Means			Significant Differences*		
Judaism Variables**	Born Jews	Partners	Converts	BJ vs. PR	BJ vs. CV	PR vs. CV
Religious Practices						
Have a Hanukah menorah*	0.99(1)	0.88(1)	0.91(1)	–		+
Belong to a Synagogue*	0.99(2)	0.64(14)	0.69(12)	–	–	–
Participate in Passover Seder	3.89(3)	3.74(2)	3.52(2)	–	–	–
Attend Yom Kippur Services	3.77(4)	3.40(6)	3.39(5)	–	–	
Have a Jewish Prayer Book*	0.93(5)	0.82(10)	0.79(6)	–	–	–
Light Hanukah Candles	3.67(6)	3.65(5)	3.40(4)	–	–	–
Have a Jewish Bible*	0.92(7)	0.78(12)	0.75(9)	–	–	
Exchange Hanukah Presents	3.68(8)	3.23(8)	3.45(3)			
Attend Rosh Hashanah Services	3.71(9)	3.34(7)	3.30(7)			
Have a *Mezzuzah* on Outside Doorway(s)*	0.90(10)	0.63(13)	0.73(10)	–	–	–
Know *Shema* in Hebrew*	0.89(11)	0.93(3)	0.77(8)		–	
Know *Kiddush* (Over Wine) in Hebrew*	0.89(12)	0.92(4)	0.68(14)		–	–
Know *Hamotzi* (Over Bread) in Hebrew*	0.89(13)	0.90(9)	0.59(15)		–	–
Know Candle Blessing in Hebrew*	0.80(14)	0.80(11)	0.70(11)		–	–*
Eat Only Unleavened Food During Passover	2.85(15)	2.38(16)	2.44(16)		–	
Fast on Yom Kippur	2.78(16)	2.81(15)	2.82(13)			
Light Sabbath Candles	2.15(17)	1.77(18)	2.15(18)	–		+
Say *Kiddush* over Wine (or Partner)	1.87(18)	1.42(20)	0.63(20)	–	–	–
Attend Purim Services	1.89(19)	1.33(21)	1.84(19)	–		+
Attend Sabbath Services	2.10(20)	1.92(17)	2.33(17)	–		+
Have a *Mezzuzah* On Inside Doorway(s)*	0.28(21)	0.32(19)	0.25(23)			
Have a Home Sabbath Service	1.56(22)	1.19(22)	1.61(21)	–		+
Observe Sukkot	1.60(23)	1.17(23)	1.59(22)	–		+

Keep Kosher at Home	1.02(24)	0.70(27)	0.94(27)			—
Have Separate Passover Dishes#	0.17(25)	0.14(24)	0.17(24)			—
Have an Active Role in Jewish Worship Services	1.21(26)	0.85(26)	0.77(29)		—	—
Refrain from Work on the Sabbath	0.71(27)	0.50(29)	1.00(26)			+
Engage in Formal Study of Judaism	1.11(28)	0.99(25)	1.24(25)		+	+
Eat Kosher Away from Home	0.72(29)	0.52(28)	0.93(28)		+	+
Attend a Daily Minyan	0.34(30)	0.21(31)	0.18(32)			
Say Daily Morning Prayers	0.30(31)	0.20(32)	0.69(30)			
Use Tefillin (or Partner)	0.25(32)	0.24(30)	0.24(31)		—	+
Total, Major Rabbinic Religious Practices##	25.41	23.35	23.81		—	—
Total, Supportive Rabbinic Religious Practices##	6.44	5.43	5.25		—	—
Importance of Religious Activities						
Live Near a Synagogue	3.03(1)	1.46(6)	2.83(4)		—	+
Continued Study of Judaism	3.02(2)	2.87(2)	3.23(2)			+
Learn to Follow the Prayers	2.86(3)	2.85(3)	3.25(1)		+	+
Learn the Prayers in Hebrew	2.82(4)	2.72(4)	3.03(3)			+
Learn Hebrew	2.54(5)	2.36(5)	2.53(5)			—
Bar or Bat Mitzvah	2.41(6)	2.93(1)	1.58(6)	+	—	—
Total, Importance of Major Rabbinic Religious Concerns##	15.75	14.52	14.61		—	—

* "—" indicates that the comparison score is significantly lower than the born Jews' score; in the case of PR vs. CV, partners represent born Jews.

"+" indicates that the comparison score is significantly higher than the born Jews' score; in the case of PR vs. CV, partners represent born Jews.

** Variables are listed within each category from highest to lowest according to the in-married, born Jew mean; bracketed number (for example, (1)) is the rank.

Some variables permit only a yes or no response (for example, having or not having a Hanukah menorah); therefore, category means are shown by the rank order as based on a collapse of the positive categories on scale items to compare with "Yes, I do" responses.

Yes or no item.

A description of the Total (scale) variables can be obtained from Dr. Forster.

TABLE 4.9
COMPARISONS AMONG BORN JEWS' (BJ), PARTNERS' (PR), AND CONVERTS' (CV) REGULAR CHRISTIAN RELIGIOUS PRACTICES

Christian Variables**	Means			Significant Differences*		
	Born Jews	Partners	Converts	BJ vs. PR	BJ vs. CV	PR vs. CV
Decorate home at Christmas/Hanukah	2.03(1)	1.95(2)	2.45(3)		+	+
Send Christmas cards	1.53(2)	1.56(4)	1.85(4)			
Exchange Christmas presents with relatives	0.99(3)	2.22(1)	3.11(1)	+	+	+
Attend a Christmas family gathering	0.69(4)	1.89(3)	2.63(2)	+	+	+
Attend a Christian service	0.50(5)	0.47(7)	0.51(7)			
Exchange Christmas presents in own household	0.27(6)	1.00(5)	1.09(6)	+	+	

Attend Easter family gatherings	0.15(7)	0.92(6)	1.43(5)	+		+
Decorate a Christmas tree	0.07(8)	0.43(8)	0.49(8)	+	+	+
Attend a Christmas service	0.05(9)	0.30(9)	0.31(9)	+	+	+
Attend Easter services	0.04(10)	0.19(10)	0.22(10)	+	+	+
Total, Christian practices*	2.44	10.90	12.39	+	+	+

* "−" indicates that the comparison score is significantly lower than the born Jews' score; in the case of PR vs. CV, partners represent born Jews.

"+" indicates that the comparison score is significantly higher than the born Jews' score; in the case of PR vs. CV, partners represent born Jews.

** Variables are listed within each category from highest to lowest according to the in-married, born Jew mean; bracketed number (for example, (1)) is the rank.

* A description of the Total (scale) variables can be obtained from Dr. Forster.

TABLE 4.10
COMPARISONS AMONG BORN JEWS' (BJ), PARTNERS' (PR), AND CONVERTS' (CV) INVOLVEMENTS IN THE JEWISH COMMUNITY

Ethnic Variables**	Means			Significant Differences*		
	Born Jews	Partners	Converts	BJ vs. PR	BJ vs. CV	PR vs. CV
Jewish Ethnic Practice						
Have Jewish art on display*	0.87(1)	0.67(1)	0.79(1)	–	–	
Watch Jewish TV or films	2.86(2)	2.25(2)	2.77(2)	–	–	+
Subscribe to a Jewish newspaper*	0.65(3)	0.38(3)	0.54(3)	–	–	+
Belong to a Jewish organization*	0.60(4)	0.27(10)	0.38(6)	–	–	
Belong to a Synagogue-related group*	0.44(5)	0.16(12)	0.28(8)	–	–	+
Read Jewishly related literature	2.21(6)	1.54(4)	2.15(4)	–	–	+
Attend Jewish groups	2.04(7)	0.98(9)	1.31(11)	–	–	+
Participate in ongoing Jewish education*	0.36(8)	0.16(11)	0.29(7)	–	–	+
Wear Jewish jewelry	1.37(9)	1.41(5)	2.00(5)	–	+	+
Listen to Jewish music	1.83(10)	1.12(8)	1.28(12)	–	–	+
Attend Jewish cultural events	1.88(12)	1.24(6)	1.65(10)	–	–	+
Serve as an officer for a Jewish organization	1.56(11)	0.55(14)	0.58(13)	–	–	
Attend Jewish lectures	1.70(13)	1.09(7)	1.65(9)	–	–	+
Belong to a YMHA or Jewish community center*	0.14(14)	0.11(13)	0.10(14)	–	–	
Teach or organize Jewish activities	1.07(15)	0.47(15)	0.52(15)	–	–	

Percent Jewish neighbors	2.14	2.27	2.54		—	—
Percent Jewish friends	75.00	54.50	45.74		—	—
Percent give to Jewish charity	67.75	61.40	63.91		—	+
Total, Jewish ethnic inputs##	9.26	6.50	8.75			
Importance of Ethnic Activities						
Support of Israel	3.58(1)	3.14(2)	2.78(3)	—	—	—
Visit to Israel	3.39(2)	3.03(3)	2.79(2)	—	—	—
Live near good public school	3.26(3)	3.39(1)	3.03(1)	—	—	—
Have a substantial number of Jewish neighbors	2.93(4)	2.64(4)	2.50(4)		—	—
Aliyah to Israel for others	2.48(5)	2.35(5)	2.17(5)		—	—
Aliyah to Israel for self	1.23(6)	1.84(6)	1.78(6)		+	+
Live near Jewish Day school	1.10(7)	1.45(7)	1.69(7)		+	+
Total, major rabbinic ethnic involvements##	13.54	12.99	12.00			—

* "—" indicates that the comparison score is significantly lower than the born Jews' scores; in the case of PR vs. CV, partners represent born Jews.

"+" indicates that the comparison score is significantly higher than the born Jews' score; in the case of PR vs. CV, partners represent born Jews.

** Variables are listed within each category from highest to lowest according to the in-married, born Jew mean; bracketed number (for example, (1)) is the rank

Some variables permit only a yes or no response (for example, having or not having a Hanukah menorah); therefore, category means are shown by the rank order as based on a collapse of the positive categories on scale items to compare with "Yes, I do" responses.

\# Yes or no item.

\#\# A description of the Total (scale) variables can be obtained from Dr. Forster.

TABLE 4.11

COMPARISONS AMONG BORN JEWS' (BJ), PARTNERS' (PR), AND CONVERTS' (CV) COMMITMENT TO JEWISH CHILD-REARING FOCUSES

	Means			Significant Differences*		
Child-Rearing Variables**	Born Jews	Partners	Converts	BJ vs. PR	BJ vs. CV	PR vs. CV
General Religious Practices						
Believing in God	2.21(1)	2.27(1)	2.63(1)		+	+
Being Free to Choose Own Religion	1.41(2)	1.93(2)	2.26(2)		+	+
Jewish Religious Practices						
A Hebrew Name	2.80(1)	2.50(2)	2.29(4)	–	–	
A Bar or Bat Mitzvah	2.76(2)	2.49(3)	2.34(2)		–	
Circumcision or Dedication	2.74(3)	2.53(1)	2.43(1)		–	
A Jewish Part-Time Education	2.69(4)	2.34(4)	2.30(3)	–	–	
Believing that Jesus was not the Messiah	2.15(5)	1.72(5)	1.70(5)	–	–	
Confirmation	2.02(6)	1.48(6)	1.50(6)	–	–	
Not Participating in School Christmas or Easter Celebration	1.45(7)	1.12(8)	1.20(8)	–	–	
A Jewish Day School Education	1.15(8)	1.44(7)	1.34(7)	+	+	
Christian Practices						
Having Positive Beliefs About Jesus' Ministry	0.28(1)	0.55(1)	0.95(1)	+	+	+

Variable							
Attending Christian Religious Services, Being Baptized							
Baptized	0.18(2)	0.43(2)	0.37(2)		+	+	+
Being Baptized	0.06(3)	0.14(3)	0.28(3)	+	+	+	+
Total, Child Christian Practices#	4.40	5.43	5.88		+	+	+
Jewish Ethnic Involvements for Children							
Having a Strong Jewish Identity	2.89(1)	2.59(1)	2.30(1)		−	−	−
Raising a Jewish Family	2.85(2)	2.49(2)	2.18(2)		−	−	−
Marrying a Jew (or Convert)	2.72(3)	1.82(5)	1.36(5)		−	−	−
Having a Few Jewish Friends	2.46(4)	2.28(3)	2.10(3)			−	
Visiting Israel	2.44(5)	1.99(4)	1.75(4)		−	−	
Dating Only Jews	2.20(6)	1.12(9)	0.89(9)		−	−	
Having Mostly Jewish Friends	2.13(7)	1.57(6)	1.31(6)		−	−	
Attending a Jewish Summer Camp	1.58(8)	1.33(7)	1.30(7)		−	−	
Study in Israel	1.43(9)	1.19(8)	1.05(8)		−	+	
Aliyah to Israel	0.75(10)	0.95(10)	1.00(10)		−	−	
Total, Child Major Jewish Involvements#	38.52	32.99	30.33		−	−	

* "—" Indicates that the comparison score is significantly lower than the born Jews' score; in the case of PR vs. CV, partners represent born Jews.
"+" indicates that the comparison score is significantly higher than the born Jews' score; in the case of PR vs. CV, partners represent born Jews.

** Variables are listed within each category from highest to lowest according to the in-married, born Jew mean; bracketed number (for example, (1)) is the rank.

A description of the Total (scale) variables can be obtained from Dr. Forster.

Bibliography

Angel, Marc D. "Another Halachic Approach to Conversion." *Tradition* (Winter-Spring 1972), 67–69.

Bamberger, Bernard J. *Proselytism in the Talmudic Period.* Cincinnati: Hebrew University College Press, 1939.

Bamberger, Bernard J. "Conversion to Judaism: Theologically Speaking." In David Max Eichhorn (ed.), *Conversion to Judaism: A History* (pp. 52–70). New York: Ktav, 1965.

Baron, Salo. *A Social and Religious History of the Jews* (Vol. 1). New York: Columbia University Press, 1952.

Berger, Graenum. "Intermarriage and the Failure of the American Jewish Community." *Proceedings of the Conference on Intermarriage and the Future of the American Jew.* New York: Commission on Synagogue Relations and Federation of Jewish Philanthropies of New York, December 1964.

Bernards, Rabbi Solomon (ed.). *Who Is A Jew? A Reader.* New York: Anti-Defamation League, 1972.

Bigman, Stanley K. *The Jewish Population of Greater Washington in 1956.* Portland: Jewish Community Council of Greater Washington, 1957.

Blatt, Serano. "Outreach." Letter to Rabbis, Temple Administrators, and Presidents. Spring 1986.

Braude, William G. *Jewish Proselytism in the First Five Centuries of the Common Era.* Providence, RI: Brown University Press, 1940.

Brodbar-Nemzer, Jay J. "Divorce and Group Commitment: The Case of the Jews." *Journal of Marriage and the Family* 48 (May 1986), 329–340.

Cardozo, Arlene Rossen. *Jewish Family Celebrations: The Sabbath, Festivals, and Ceremonies.* New York: St. Martin's, 1982.

Carmel, Abraham. "My Chosen People." *Tradition* 2 (Winter 1988), 15–27.

Cowan, Paul, and Cowan, Rachel. "Interfaith Couples: A Delicate Imbalance." *Hadassah* (October 1987), 22–25.

Cowan, Paul, and Cowan, Rachel. *Mixed Blessings: Marriage Between Jews and Christians.* New York: Doubleday, 1987.

Davis, Moshe. "Mixed Marriages in Western Jewry." *Jewish Journal of Sociology* (December 1968), 179–186.

Diamant, Anita. *The New Jewish Wedding.* New York: Summit, 1985.

Donin, Rabbi Hayim Halevy. *To Be A Jew: A Guide to Jewish Observance in Contemporary Life.* New York: Basic Books, 1972.

Dresner, Samuel H., and Sherwin, Bryon L. *Judaism: The Way of Sanctification.* New York: United Synagogue, 1978.

Edelheit, Joseph A. "Are We Ready for the New Jewish Community?" *Journal of Reform Judaism* (Winter 1957), 79–86.

Edelheit, Joseph A. *An Introduction to Judaism* (Course Outline). Chicago: Chicago Association of Reform Rabbis and Chicago Region Rabbinical Assembly, 1980.

Eichhorn, David Max (ed.). *Conversion to Judaism: A History and Analysis.* New York: Ktav, 1965.

Franzblau, Abraham N. "Conversion to Judaism: Psychologically Speaking." In *Conversion to Judaism: A History and Analysis* (pp. 189–202). New York: Ktav, 1965.

Friedman, Peter. "The Who, Whats, and Wheres of Jewish Chicago." *JUF News* (April 1986), 34–37.

Gallob, Ben. "Encourage Converts to Judaism in Interfaith Marriages, Urges Author." *Sentinel* (November 21, 1985), 20.

Gallob, Ben. "Cause of Conflict in Mixed Marriages Is Ethnic As Well As Religious-Based." *Sentinel* (March 6, 1986), 25.

Gallob, Ben. "Jews by Choice: Can They Meet the Expectations of Their Jewish Mate?" *Sentinel* (September 25, 1986), 21.

Gallob, Ben. "Jewish Conversion on Rise in U.S., Is No Longer a Topic to be Avoided." *Sentinel* (January 29, 1987), 26–27.

Gallob, Ben. "When One Spouse Chooses to Convert to Judaism. . . . in a Gentile Marriage." *Sentinel* (April 16, 1987), 47.

Gallob, Ben. "Intermarriage Reported to be Far More Likely Among Younger Jews." *Sentinel* (November 24, 1988), 27–29.

Gallob, Ben. "New Converts to Judaism Are Not Always White with European Roots." *Sentinel* (January 11, 1990), 22B.

Ginzberg, Louis. *The Legends of the Jews* (Vol. 4). New York: Jewish Publication Society, 1941.

Glazer, Nathan. "Jews and Intermarriage." *Sentinel* (June 25, 1987), 14.

Goldenberg, Naomi Ruth. "A Response to Anne Roiphe on the Jewish Family: The Problem of Intermarriage." *Tikkun* 2(1), 118–119.

Goldscheider, Calvin. "Social Change and Jewish Continuity." In Richard T. Schaefer and Robert P. Lamm (eds.), *Introducing Sociology: A Collection of Readings* (pp. 278–280). New York: McGraw-Hill, 1987.

Goldscheider, Calvin, and Zuckerman, Alan S. *The Transformation of the Jews*. Chicago: University of Chicago Press, 1984.

Goldstein, Sidney. "Population Trends in American Jewry." *Judaism* 36 (Spring 1987), 135–146.

Goldstein, Sidney, and Goldscheider, Calvin. *Jewish Americans: Three Generations in a Jewish Community*. Englewood Cliffs, NJ: Prentice-Hall, 1968.

Gordis, Robert. *Judaism in a Christian World*. New York: Free Press, 1966.

Gordon, Albert Isaac. *The Nature of Conversion*. Boston: Beacon Press, 1967.

Graetz, Heinrich. *History of the Jews*. Philadelphia: Jewish Publication Society, 1949.

Greenberg, Blu. *How to Run a Traditional Jewish Household*. New York: Simon & Schuster, 1983.

Gruzen, Lee F. *Raising Your Jewish/Christian Child*. New York: Dodd, Mead, 1987.

Harlow, Jules (ed. and trans.). *Siddur Sim Shalom*. New York: United Synagogue of America, 1985.

Harris, Monford. *On Entering Jewish Existence: Towards a Theology of Conversion*. Unpublished manuscript. Chicago: Spertus College of Judaica, 1970.

Hartman, David. *A Living Covenant: The Innovative Spirit in Traditional Judaism*. New York: Free Press, 1985.

Helfgott, Esther Altshol. "A Convert's View of Jewish Men and Women." *JUF News* (September 1987), 78.

Herberg, Will. *Judaism and Modern Man: An Interpretation of Jewish Religion*. New York: Atheneum, 1970.

Herman, Simon N. *Jewish Identity: A Social-Psychological Perspective*. Beverly Hills, CA: Sage, 1977.

Hertz, Joseph H. (ed.). *The Pentateuch and Haftorahs*. London: Soncino Press, 1938.

Hertzberg, Arthur. "Modern Judaism and the Emancipation: A Reassessment After 2 Centuries." *Modern Judaism* 1 (1946), 1–19.

Heschel, Abraham Joshua. *God in Search of Man: A Philosophy of Judaism.* New York: Farrar, Straus, & Giroux, 1955.

Hierich, H. "Change of Heart: A Test of Some Widely Held Theories about Religious Conversion." *American Journal of Sociology* 83 (1977), 653–679.

Hirsh, Rabbi Richard. "Confronting the 'December Dilemma': Intermarried Families and the Holidays." *Sentinel* (December 25, 1986), 29, 31.

Huberman, Stephen. "Conversion to Judaism: An Analysis of Family Matters." *Judaism* (Summer 1981), 312–321.

Huberman, Stephen. "From Christianity to Judaism: Religion Changes in American Society." *Conservative Judaism* 36 (Fall 1982), 20–28.

Jacobs, Louis. *A Jewish Theology.* New York: Behrman, 1983.

Jakobovits, Immanuel. "The Timely and Timeless." *Tradition* (Spring 1989), 164–215.

Kalb, Harold, and Weinshanker, Jack. "Conservative Movement Milestone: Joint Conference Intermarriage and Conversion." *United Synagogue Review* (Fall 1987), 6, 24.

Kaplan, Mordecai. *Judiasm as a Civilization.* New York: Macmillan, 1957. (Original work published in 1934.)

Katz, Jacob. *Exclusiveness and Tolerance.* London: Oxford University Press, 1961.

Kaufmann, Yehezkel. *The Religion of Israel* (trans. and abridged by Moshe Greenberg). Chicago: University of Chicago Press, 1960.

Kertzer, Rabbi Morris N. *What Is A Jew?* (4th ed.). New York: Collier, 1978.

Kukoff, Lydia. *Choosing Judaism.* New York: Union of American Hebrew Congregations, 1981.

Lerner, Rabbi Stephen C. "Jews by Choice." *Rabbinical Assembly Proceedings* 45 (1983), 71–76.

Levenson, Alan. "Reform Attitudes, in the Past, Toward Intermarriage." *Judaism* 38 (Summer 1989), 320–332.

Levin, Michael Graubart. *Journey to Tradition: Odyssey of a Born-Again Jew.* New York: Ktav, 1986.

Lieberman, S. Zevulun. "Syrian Jews." *Tradition* 23 (Spring 1988), 27–52.

Linzer, Norman. *The Jewish Family: Authority and Tradition in Modern Perspective.* New York: Human Sciences Press, 1984.

Mayer, Egon. "A Cure for Intermarriage?" *Moneit* 4, 6 (June 1979), 62–64.

Mayer, Egon. *Children of Intermarriage: A Study in Patterns of Identification and Family Life.* New York: American Jewish Committee, 1983.

Mayer, Egon. "Jews by Choice: Their Impact on the Contemporary American Jewish Community." *Rabbinical Assembly Proceedings* 45 (1983), 57–70.

Mayer, Egon. *Achieving Identity in an Ascriptive Community: The Dilemma of Conversion in Modern Judaism.* Unpublished manuscript. New York: Brooklyn College, 1984.

Mayer, Egon. *Love and Tradition: Marriage Between Jews and Christians.* New York: Plenum, 1985.

Mayer, Egon. "From Outrage to Outreach: Alternative Jewish Responses to Intermarriage." *Outlook* (Fall 1987), 12–13.

Mayer, Egon, and Augar, Amy. *Conversion Among the Intermarried: Choosing to Become Jewish.* New York: American Jewish Committee, 1987.

Mayer, Egon, and Sheingold, Carl. *Intermarriages and the Jewish Future: A National Study in Summary.* New York: American Jewish Committee, 1979.

Minkin, Jacob S. *The Shaping of the Modern Mind.* New York: Thomas Yoselott Press, 1963.

Moore, George Foote. *Judaism in the First Centuries of the Christian Era: The Age of the Tannaim.* Cambridge, MA: Harvard University Press, 1927.

Netter, Perry. "Will Your God Really Be My God?" *Moment* (January/February 1989), 44–47.

Petsonk, Judy, and Rensen, Jim. *The Intermarriage Handbook: A Guide for Jews and Christians.* New York: Arbor, 1988.

Petuchowski, Jacob J. "Realism About Mixed Marriages." *CCAR Journal* (October 1966), 35–40.

"Proselytes." *Encyclopedia Judaica* (pp. 1182–1194). New York: MacMillian, 1972.

Rabbi's Manual. New York: Rabbinical Assembly of America, 1965.

Rosenman, Yehuda. "The Jewish Family: Lights and Shadows." *Judaism* 36 (Spring 1987), 147–153.

Rosenthal, Erich. "Studies of Jewish Intermarriage in the U.S." In Morris Fine and Milton Himmelfarb (eds.), *American Jewish*

Yearbook, 1963 (pp. 3–71) New York: American Jewish Committee, 1963.

Rozwaski, Chaim Z. "Jewish Law and Intermarriage." *Jewish Life* (July/August 1969), 18–23.

Rubenstein, Richard L. "Intermarriage and Conversion on the American College Campus." In Werener J. Cahnman (ed.), *Intermarriage and Jewish Life*. New York: Shocken, 1963.

Sandberg, Neil C. *Jewish Life in Los Angeles: A Window to Tomorrow*. New York: Lanhainm, 1986.

Schechter, Solomon. *Aspects of Rabbinic Theology*. New York: Shocken, 1981. (Original work published in 1909.)

Schneider, Susan Weidman. "Review: Love and Tradition: Marriage Between Jews and Christians." *United Synagogue Review* (Spring 1987), 32.

Schwartz, Arnold. "Intermarriage in the U.S." In Morris Fine, Milton Himmelfarb, and Martha Jelenko (eds.), *American Jewish Yearbook 1970* (pp. 101–121). New York: American Jewish Committee, 1970.

Sherwin, Byron. *Mystical Theology and Social Dissent: The Life and Works of Judah Lowe of Prague*. Rutherford, NJ: Fairleigh-Dickenson University Press, 1982.

Silberman, Charles. *A Certain People: American Jews and Their Lives Today*. New York: Simon & Schuster, 1985.

Silverstein, Rabbi Alan. "Project Joseph: Responding to Intermarriage." *Outlook* (Fall 1987), 14–15.

Sklare, Marshall. "Intermarriage and Jewish Survival." *Commentary* 49, 3 (March 1970), 51–58.

Sklare, Marshall. *America's Jews*. New York: Random House, 1971.

Sklare, Marshall, and Greenblum, Joseph. *Jewish Identity on the Suburban Frontier* (2nd ed.). Chicago: University of Chicago Press, 1979.

Soloveichik, Joseph B. "Beyn Brisk L'Boston" [Between Brisk and Boston]. *Hadoar* (September 5, 1986), 5–9.

Stern, Malcolm H. "Jewish Marriage and Intermarriage in the Federal Period (1776–1840)." *American Jewish Archives* 19 (November 1967), 142–143.

Strassfeld, Michael. *The Jewish Holidays: A Guide and Commentary*. New York: Harper and Row, 1985.

Straus, Roger A. "Religious Conversion as a Personal and Collective Accomplishment." *Sociological Analysis* 40, 2 (1979), 158–165.

Tobin, Gary. "Understanding and Dealing with the Reasons for Intermarriage." *JUF News* (July 1990), 48, 63.

Ullman, Chana. "Cognitive and Emotional Antecedents of Religious Conversions." *Journal of Personality and Social Behavior* 43, 1 (1982), 183–192.

Waxman, Chaim I. *America's Jews in Transition.* Philadelphia: Temple University Press, 1983.

Waxman, Ruth B. (ed.). "How the Emancipation and the Enlightenment Changed Jewish History." *Judaism* 38, 44 (Fall 1989).

Winkler, Gershon. "Intermarriage: What If It's Too Late?" *Jewish Homemaker* (April–May, 1986), 5–7.

Yearbook, Conference of American Rabbis, XIX. New York: Central Conference of American Rabbis, 1909.